Here's what people are saying about
the DOING LIFE TOGETHER Series . . .

Small Group Members Are Saying...

Six weeks ago we were strangers. Today we are a family in Christ. We talk to each other, lean on each other, encourage each other, and hold each other accountable. We have gone from meeting as a Bible study to getting together for several social events, meeting for Sunday services, and organizing service projects in our community.

—Sandy and Craig

The Purpose-Driven material quickly moved us beyond group and closer toward family, beyond reading God's Word to knowing God!

—The Coopers

Small Group Leaders Are Saying...

Even though our group has been together for several years, the questions in this study have allowed us to connect on a much deeper level. Many of the men are displaying emotions we haven't seen before.

—Steve and Jennifer

The material has become a personal compass to me. When I find myself needing to make a decision, I ask, "Does it bring me closer to God's family? Does it make me more like Christ? Am I using the gifts God gave me? Am I sharing God's love? Am I surrendering my life to please God?" I still have a long way to go, but this has been a blessing and a compass to keep me on his path.

—Craig

Pastors and Church Leaders Are Saying...

We took the entire church through this curriculum, and the results were nothing less than miraculous. Our congregation was ignited with passion for God and his purposes for our lives. It warmed up the entire congregation as we grew closer to God by "Doing Life Together."

—Kerry

The Purpose-Driven format helped our groups realize there are some areas that they are doing very well in (fellowship and discipleship) and other areas that they need to do some work in. What is amazing is to see how they are committing to work on these areas (especially evangelism and ministry).

—Steve

Other Studies in the DOING LIFE TOGETHER Series

Beginning Life Together (God's Purposes for Your Life)

Connecting with God's Family (Fellowship)

Growing to Be Like Christ (Discipleship)

Developing Your SHAPE to Serve Others (Ministry)

Sharing Your Life Mission Every Day (Evangelism)

After you complete this study, we'd love to hear how DOING LIFE TOGETHER has affected your life, your group, or your church! Write us at stories@lifetogether.com. You can also log on to www.lifetogether.com to see how others are putting "life together" into practice.

SURRENDERING YOUR
LIFE FOR GOD'S PLEASURE

six sessions on
worship

written by
BRETT and DEE EASTMAN
TODD and DENISE WENDORFF
KAREN LEE-THORP

ZONDERVAN™

GRAND RAPIDS, MICHIGAN 49530 USA

ZONDERVAN™

Surrendering Your Life for God's Pleasure
Copyright © 2002 by Brett and Deanna Eastman, Todd and Denise Wendorff,
and Karen Lee-Thorp

Requests for information should be addressed to:

Zondervan, *Grand Rapids, Michigan 49530*

ISBN 0-310-24677-6

Interior icons by Tom Clark

Printed in the United States of America

06 07 08 09 10 • 30 29 28 27 26 25 24 23 22 21 20

CONTENTS

Foreword   7
Acknowledgments   9
Read Me First   11

SESSION 1   Becoming a Worshiper   15
SESSION 2   How Big Is Your God?   24
SESSION 3   Surrendering Your Past   33
SESSION 4   Surrendering Your Future   42
SESSION 5   Surrendering Your Substitutes   51
SESSION 6   The Crown of Life   59

FREQUENTLY ASKED QUESTIONS   65

APPENDIX
    Purpose-Driven Group Agreement   67
    Small Group Calendar   68
    Purpose Team Roles   70
    Purpose-Driven Life Health Assessment   72
    Purpose-Driven Life Health Plan   74
    Spiritual Partners' Check-In Page   77
    Serving Communion   78
    Memory Verses   80
    Daily Devotional Readings   81
    Prayer and Praise Report   82
    Sample Journal Page   84

LEADERSHIP TRAINING
    Small Group Leadership 101   85
        (Top Ten Ideas for New Facilitators)
    Small Group Leadership Lifters   88
        (Weekly Leadership Tips)
    Leader's Notes   93

About the Authors   107
Small Group Roster   108

FOREWORD

Over twenty-five years ago I noticed a little phrase in Acts 13:36 that forever altered the direction of my life. It read, *"David had served God's purpose in his own generation."* I was fascinated by that simple yet profound summary of David's life, and I determined to make it the goal of my life, too. I would seek to discover and fulfill the purposes for which God had created me.

This decision provoked a number of questions: What are God's purposes for putting us on earth? What does a purpose-driven life look like? How can the church enable people to fulfill God's eternal purposes? I read through the Bible again and again, searching for the answers to these questions. As a direct result of what I learned, my wife, Kay, and I decided to start Saddleback Church and build it from the ground up on God's five purposes for us (which are found in the New Testament).

In the living laboratory of Saddleback Church, we were able to experiment with different ways to help people understand, apply, and live out the purposes of God. I've written two books about the lessons we've learned (*The Purpose-Driven Church* and, more recently, *The Purpose-Driven Life*). As other churches became interested in what we were doing, we began sharing the tools, programs, and studies we developed at Saddleback. Over a million copies of *The Purpose-Driven Church* are now in print in some nineteen languages, and The Purpose-Driven Class Curriculum (Class 101–401) is now used in tens of thousands of churches around the world. We hope that the same will be true for this exciting new small group curriculum.

DOING LIFE TOGETHER is a groundbreaking study in several ways. It is the first small group curriculum built completely on the purpose-driven paradigm. This is not just another study to be used *in* your church; it is a study *on* the church to help *strengthen* your church. Many small group curricula today are quite self-focused and individualistic. They generally do not address the importance of the local church and our role in it as believers. Another unique feature of this curriculum is its balance. In every session, the five purposes of God are stressed in some way.

But the greatest reason I am excited about releasing this DOING LIFE TOGETHER curriculum is that I've seen the dramatic changes it produces in the lives of those who study it. These small group studies were not developed in some detached ivory tower or academic setting but in the day-to-day ministry of Saddleback Church, where thousands of people meet weekly in small groups that are committed to fulfilling God's purposes. This curriculum has been tested and retested, and the results have been absolutely amazing. Lives have been changed, marriages saved, and families strengthened. And our church has grown—in the past seven years we've seen over 9,100 new believers baptized at Saddleback. I attribute these results to the fact that so many of our members are serious about living healthy, balanced, purpose-driven lives.

It is with great joy and expectation that I introduce this resource to you. I am so proud of our development team on this project: Brett and Dee Eastman, Todd and Denise Wendorff, and Karen Lee-Thorp. They have committed hundreds of hours to write, teach, develop, and refine these lessons —with much feedback along the way. This has been a labor of love, as they have shared our dream of helping you serve God's purpose in your own generation. The church will be enriched for eternity as a result.

Get ready for a life-changing journey. God bless!

—Pastor Rick Warren

Pastor Rick Warren is the author of *The Purpose-Driven Church* and *The Purpose-Driven Life* [www.purposedrivenlife.com].

ACKNOWLEDGMENTS

Sometimes in life God gives you a dream. Most of the time it remains only a dream. But every once in a while, a dream captures your heart, consumes your thoughts, and compels you to action. However, if others around you aren't motivated to share the dream and aren't moved to action along with you, it remains just that—a dream. By the grace of God and a clear call on the hearts of a few, our dream has become a reality.

The DOING LIFE TOGETHER series was birthed one summer in the hearts of Brett and Dee Eastman and Todd and Denise Wendorff, two Saddleback Church staff couples. They hoped to launch a new one-year Bible study based on the Purpose-Driven® life. They called it *The Journey: Experiencing the Transformed Life*. *The Journey* was launched with a leadership team that committed its heart and soul to the project. We will never be able to express our gratitude to each of you who shared the dream and helped to continue the dream now, three years later.

Early on, Karen Lee-Thorp, an experienced writer of many Bible studies, joined the team. Oh, God, you are good to us!

Saddleback pastors and staff members too numerous to mention have supported our dream and have come alongside to fan the flames. We would have never gotten this off the ground without their belief and support.

We also want to express our overwhelming gratitude to the numerous ministries and churches that helped shape our spiritual heritage. We're particularly grateful for Bill Bright of Campus Crusade for Christ, who gave us a dream for reaching the world, and for Bill Hybels of Willow Creek Community Church, who gave us a great love and respect for the local church.

Our special thanks goes to Pastor Rick and Kay Warren for sharing the dream of a healthy and balanced purpose-driven church that produces purpose-driven lives over time. It clearly is the basis for the body of this work. God only knows how special you are to us and how blessed we feel to be a part of your team.

Finally, we thank our beloved families who have lived with us, laughed at us, and loved us through it all. We love doing our lives together with you.

READ ME FIRST
DOING LIFE TOGETHER

D OING LIFE TOGETHER is unique in that it was designed in community for community. Four of us have been doing life together, in one way or another, for over fifteen years. We have been in a small group together, done ministry together, and been deeply involved in each other's lives. We have shared singleness, marriage, childbirth, family loss, physical ailments, teenage years, job loss, and, yes, even marital problems.

Our community has not been perfect, but it has been real. We have made each other laugh beyond belief, cry to the point of exhaustion, feel as grateful as one can imagine, and get so mad we couldn't see straight. We've said things we will always regret and shared moments we will never forget, but through it all we have discovered a diamond in the rough—a community that increasingly reflects the character of Jesus Christ. God has used our relationships with each other to deepen our understanding of and intimacy with him. We have come to believe that we cannot fully experience the breadth and depth of the purpose-driven life outside of loving relationships in the family of God (Ephesians 2:19–22; 4:11–13).

Doing life together was God's plan from the beginning of time. From the relationships of Father, Son, and Holy Spirit in the Trinity, to the twelve apostles, to the early house churches, and even Jesus' final words in the Great Commission (Matthew 28:16–20)—all share the pattern of life together. God longs to connect all of his children in loving relationships that cultivate the five biblical purposes of the church deep within their hearts. With this goal in mind, we have created the DOING LIFE TOGETHER series—the first purpose-driven small group series.

The series is designed to walk you and your group down a path, six weeks at a time over the course of a year, to help you do the purpose-driven life together. There are six study guides in this series. You can study them individually, or you can follow the one-year path through the six studies. *Beginning Life Together* offers a six-week overview of the purpose-driven life. The other five guides (*Connecting with God's Family, Growing to Be Like Christ, Developing Your SHAPE to Serve Others, Sharing Your Life Mission Every Day,* and *Surrendering Your Life for God's Pleasure*) each explore one of the five purposes of the church more deeply.

In his book *The Purpose-Driven Life*, Rick Warren invites you to commit to live a purpose-driven life every day. The DOING LIFE TOGETHER series was designed to help you live this purpose-driven life through being part of a purpose-driven small group. A purpose-driven group doesn't simply connect people in community or grow people through Bible study. These groups seek to help each member balance all five biblical purposes of the church. The fivefold purpose of a healthy group parallels the fivefold purpose of the church.

Victory through Surrender

At this moment, as you are reading these words, a battle is being waged. God is battling to win your heart. He is battling to free it from all that urges you to mistrust him. God, the all-powerful Maker of all that is, will not take your allegiance by force. He wants your heart willingly, or not at all.

Perhaps you've already said yes to God: "Yes, you deserve to be the captain of my soul because you are good and wise and strong and beautiful. Yes, I will follow you wherever you lead." Yet, each hour and day confronts you with a new opportunity to say yes or no to your captain. Each hour and day he battles for your heart anew, not against you but alongside you. And your role in the battle is, paradoxically, not to fight but to consent as *he* fights. Your role is to surrender, adore, consent, and do as he bids.

This role doesn't come easily to anyone. You may be the sort of person who prefers to be in charge rather than take orders. Or you may prefer to be passive and let others make decisions, but you flinch when to follow God's instructions means to stand up to people or to risk your own security. Either way, entrusting your life to God goes against your instincts.

That's why *surrender* and *worship* are almost two words for the same act. Worship celebrates the here-and-now presence of our good, wise, strong, and beautiful God. Worship is an act of surrender to this Present One, and daily surrender to his instructions is the supreme act of worship. Worship and surrender are the wellspring of life together with God and his people.

Outline of Each Session

Most people desire to live a purpose-driven life, but few people actually achieve this on a consistent basis. That's why we've included elements of all five purposes in every meeting—so that you can live a healthy, balanced spiritual life over time.

When you see the following symbols in this book, you will know that the questions and exercises in that section promote that particular purpose.

 CONNECTING WITH GOD'S FAMILY (FELLOWSHIP). The foundation for spiritual growth is an intimate connection with God and his family. The questions in this section will help you get to know the members of your small group so that you'll begin to feel a sense of belonging. This section is designed to open your time together and provide a fun way to share your personal stories with one another.

 GROWING TO BE LIKE CHRIST (DISCIPLESHIP). This is the most exciting portion of each lesson. Each week you'll study one or two core passages from the Bible. The focus will be on how the truths from God's Word make a difference in your lives. We will often provide an experiential exercise to enable you not just to talk about the truth but also to experience it in a practical way.

 DEVELOPING YOUR SHAPE TO SERVE OTHERS (MINISTRY). Most people want to know how God has uniquely shaped them for ministry and where they can serve in the center of his will. This section will help make that desire a reality. Every other week or so you will be encouraged to take practical steps in developing who God uniquely made you to be in order to serve him and others better.

 SHARING YOUR LIFE MISSION EVERY DAY (EVANGELISM). Many people skip over this aspect of the Christian life because it's scary, relationally awkward, or simply too much work for their busy schedules. We understand, because we have these thoughts as well. But God calls all of us to reach out a hand to people who don't know him. It's much easier to take practical, manageable steps that can be integrated naturally into everyday life if you take them together. Every other week or so you will have an opportunity to take a small step.

 SURRENDERING YOUR LIFE FOR GOD'S PLEASURE (WORSHIP). A surrendered heart is what pleases God most. Each small group session will give you a chance to surrender your heart to God and one another in prayer. In addition, you'll be introduced to several forms of small group worship, including listening to worship CDs, singing together, reading psalms, and participating in Communion. This portion of your meeting will transform your life in ways you never thought possible. If you're new to praying in a small group, you won't be pressed to pray aloud until you feel ready.

STUDY NOTES. This section provides background notes on the Bible passage(s) you examine in the GROWING section. You may want to refer to these notes during your study.

FOR FURTHER STUDY. This section can help your more spiritually mature members take the session one step further each week on their own. If your group is ready for deeper study or is comfortable doing homework, this section and the following two sections will help you get there. You may want to encourage them to read these passages and reflect on them in a personal journal or in the Notes section at the end of each session.

MEMORY VERSES. For those group members who want to take a step of hiding God's Word in their hearts, there are six memory verses on page 80 that correspond to each weekly lesson. You may want to tear out this page and cut the verses into wallet- or purse-size cards for easy access.

PURPOSE-DRIVEN LIFE READING PLAN. This plan for reading *The Purpose-Driven Life* by Rick Warren parallels the weekly sessions in this study guide. *The Purpose-Driven Life* is the perfect complement to the DOING LIFE TOGETHER series. If your group wants to apply the material taught in the book, you can simply read the recommended piece each week, write a reflection, and discuss the teaching as a group or in pairs.

DAILY DEVOTIONS. One of the easiest ways for your group to grow together is to encourage each other to read God's Word on a regular basis. It's so much easier to stay motivated in this area if you have one another's support. On page 81 is a daily reading plan that parallels the study and helps you deepen your walk with God. There are five readings per week. If you really want to grow, we suggest you pair up with a friend (spiritual partner) to encourage each other throughout the week. Decide right now, and write the name of someone you'd like to join with for the next six weeks.

BECOMING
A WORSHIPER

I would love to stride into church on a Sunday morning with the joy of surrender welling up from my inner being. It rarely happens. More often than not, I've been driving a carful of kids while combing their hair and insisting that they wolf down some breakfast. I am frequently late, so I rush, slightly sweating, into the worship service. The first song helps me begin to corral my thoughts and aim them in the general direction of God. I have to decide to put everything else aside and make this time be about *him*. The song lyrics remind me what my life is about—*life together* with my magnificent Lord. By the third song, I'm aware that God is doing something in my heart. Peace fills me. God's majesty transcends my life's chaotic details. I have become a worshiper.

—Denise

CONNECTING WITH GOD'S FAMILY   15 min.

1. When have you had a great worship experience? (It's okay to respond, "Never.") What made it great?

2. It's important for every group to agree on a set of shared values. If your group doesn't already have an agreement (sometimes called a covenant), turn to page 67. Even if you've been together for some time and your values are clear, the Purpose-Driven Group Agreement can help your group achieve greater health and balance. We recommend that you especially consider rotating group leadership, setting up spiritual partners, and introducing purpose teams into the group. Simply go over the values and expectations listed in the agreement to be sure everyone in the group understands and accepts them. Make any necessary decisions about such issues as refreshments and child care.

GROWING TO BE LIKE CHRIST   25 min.

Worship is central to our life together with God. Yet discussions of worship often revolve around aesthetic taste. One person likes hymns, another prefers praise songs, another goes for cutting-edge music, and a fourth likes silence. Formal or informal, in a church or on a mountaintop—we all have preferences. But the words, the music, and the setting are secondary. Worship begins with an *attitude* of our hearts before God. The apostle Paul describes worship like this:

> *Therefore, I urge you, brothers, in view of God's mercy, to offer your bodies as living sacrifices, holy and pleasing to God— this is your spiritual act of worship. ²Do not conform any longer to the pattern of this world, but be transformed by the renewing of your mind. Then you will be able to test and approve what God's will is—his good, pleasing and perfect will.*
> —Romans 12:1–2

3. Worship is motivated by an awareness of "God's mercy" (verse 1). What is mercy?

How has God shown you mercy?

4. Worship begins as you "offer your bodies as living sacrifices." What picture comes to mind when you imagine offering your body in this way?

5. What does your body have to do with it? Why doesn't Paul say, "Offer your heart"?

6. Worship comes to fulfillment as you do what Paul describes in verse 2. What does it look like when someone conforms to the pattern of this world?

7. What are the signs that you are being "transformed by the renewing of your mind"?

8. What is one area of pleasing God that would be a new act of worship for you?

9. What is the connection between the kind of worship you've been discussing and the kind that goes on in a church building?

SURRENDERING YOUR LIFE FOR GOD'S PLEASURE   30 min.

Paul envisions worship as an all-day-long surrender to the will of a merciful God. The acts we normally think of as worship—singing, celebrating, and so on—are meant to train our hearts for this all-day-long surrender. Praise prepares us for surrender.

Praise is acknowledging a good quality in something. We can praise an actor for his talent, an athlete for her strength, a teacher for his insights. Similarly, we can praise God for his good qualities—faithfulness, justice, power, or wisdom. Worship goes beyond praise. Worship is acknowledging someone or something as the ultimate source of good, of life itself. Therefore, while people can deserve praise, only God deserves worship. Praise acknowledges value; worship says, "You have the highest value."

Another difference is that praise is a one-way compliment, while worship is a two-way interaction. Worship happens when we let God catch us up in the marvel of who he is, and we taste the intimacy of *eternal life together* with God. Praising God is a way of warming ourselves up for this worship connection that fuels our all-day-long surrender.

10. The psalms are the song lyrics for Israel's worship. You can use the psalms' words to expand your praise vocabulary. Read the following psalm aloud in unison. Afterward, allow some time for group members to offer their own words of praise to God in response to the psalm. Pick phrases from the psalm that are especially meaningful to you, and expand on them.

> *Come, let us sing for joy to the LORD;*
> > *let us shout aloud to the Rock of our salvation.*
> *²Let us come before him with thanksgiving*
> > *and extol him with music and song.*
>
> *³For the LORD is the great God,*
> > *the great King above all gods.*
> *⁴In his hand are the depths of the earth,*
> > *and the mountain peaks belong to him.*
> *⁵The sea is his, for he made it,*
> > *and his hands formed the dry land.*
>
> *⁶Come, let us bow down in worship,*
> > *let us kneel before the LORD our Maker;*
> *⁷for he is our God*
> > *and we are the people of his pasture,*
> > *the flock under his care.*
> > > —Psalm 95:1–7

11. You're more likely to spend your day in an attitude of worship if you spend a few minutes thinking about God and listening to God. Reading a portion of the Bible will help you do this. On page 81 you'll find a list of brief passages for daily devotions—five per week for the six weeks of this study. If you've never spent daily time with God, this is an easy way to begin. Would you consider taking on this habit for the duration of this study? See page 84 for a sample journal page that you can use as a guide for your daily devotions.

    If you're already consistent in daily devotions, consider acquiring the habit of Scripture memory. Six memory verses are provided on page 80—one verse per week. Would you consider accepting the challenge to memorize one verse per week and hide God's Word in your heart? We urge you to pair up with another person for encouragement and accountability.

12. Allow everyone to answer this question: "How can we pray for you this week?"

    Take some time to pray for these requests. Anyone who isn't used to praying aloud should feel free to offer prayers in silence.

13. You probably know someone who would appreciate being invited to join your small group. Pull an open chair into the circle. This chair represents someone you could invite to join your group.

Who could that person be? Think about family members, friends, neighbors, parents of your kids' friends, church members, coworkers, and the persons who share your hobbies. Take a moment now to prayerfully list one or two names, and then share the names with your group.

_____   _____
            NAME   NAME

Commit to

- making the call this week. Why not?—over 50 percent of those invited to a small group say yes! You may even want to invite him or her to ride with you.
- calling your church office to get the names of new members, and inviting new members who live near you to visit your group.
- serving your group by praying for and welcoming new people to your group.

STUDY NOTES

Mercy. Mercy is receiving better treatment than we deserve. Paul has spent eleven chapters in his letter to the Romans detailing how God has shown us mercy. The more aware we are that God has been incredibly merciful in rescuing us from the consequences of our folly, the more motivated we will be to offer our lives to him. The more blasé we are, thinking that we aren't that bad and that life owes us a pain-free existence, the less motivated we will be.

Bodies. Our mouths that speak encouragement or gossip, our hands that build or destroy, our eyes that watch children at play or movies on television, our ears that listen, our brains that think, our feet that set out on our destination, our sexual desires, our ambitions, our health, our physical appearance, our manly strength, our pregnant or empty wombs. The members of the culture of Paul's day were inclined to think that only the soul was of interest to the gods, but Paul insisted that worship cannot be merely inward and mystical.

Living sacrifices. Paul's original readers were familiar with the daily sight of a priest placing a living animal on an altar, killing it, and doing various ritual things with the meat and blood. Some rites (such as those of the goddess Cybele in Ephesus) involved the offering of human body parts. The worship of Jesus Christ sweeps all this away but replaces it with a self-offering that is no less drastic.

Conform. To allow a fallen human culture to force us into its mold. To care more about what others think than about what God thinks. To reflect the current signs of the times rather than the character of God's kingdom.

Transformed. The Greek for this word gives us our word *metamorphosis*, the process of being changed from one "form" to another. God wants to break us out of the world's mold so that we can become very different kinds of persons in the mold of Jesus Christ. The key to being transformed is allowing God's Word to renew our minds and to unfog our perceptions of reality.

☐ *For Further Study* on this topic, read Revelation 15:4; Psalm 2:11; Joshua 24:14–18.

☐ **Weekly Memory Verse:** Romans 12:1

☐ **The Purpose-Driven Life Reading Plan:** Day 8

NOTES

If you're using the DVD along with this curriculum, please use this space to take notes on the teaching for this session.

HOW BIG IS YOUR GOD?

Years ago I hit a spiritual slump and couldn't seem to climb out of it. I had gone through a discouraging job experience and felt as though I would never recover. Nothing I did worked. God seemed a million miles away. Day after day I would write in my journal, "God, are you even there?" I read the book of Job and kept placing my own name in Job's place. I read a dozen wise books and took counsel from numerous people who said all the right things. But nothing pierced the fog in my soul.

Then one morning the truth broke through my fog. I woke up about 4:00 A.M., wide-awake. I got up and went into my home office. I opened my Bible. Eventually I found myself reading Proverbs 3:5–6: "Trust in the LORD with all your heart and lean not on your own understanding; in all your ways acknowledge him, and he will make your paths straight." In that instant I sensed God saying to me, "You're going to be okay. I'm here, and I care about you. I am near, not distant, even when you don't feel my presence." None of this was new information, but it was finally more than information. It was God himself.

—Todd

CONNECTING WITH GOD'S FAMILY   10 min.

1. If you were God, what is one thing on earth you would address right away?

Most of us can think of a long list of things we wish God would do. But so often he doesn't take our advice! Maybe that's why some of us spend so much energy trying to handle things he seems to be overlooking. Meanwhile, others of us hang back from taking action because we don't trust God to come through with his piece of the job. For both of these reasons, trusting God to run both the universe and our personal lives is an essential step in the surrendered life. We need to become convinced, deep in our guts, that he really is faithful enough, powerful enough, and wise enough to do his job. We need to know that he's BIG—and that he knows what is best for our lives, loves us even more than we love ourselves, and has a plan for all eternity.

What is God really like? This psalmist praises the God he knows:

> *I will exalt you, my God the King;*
>> *I will praise your name for ever and ever.*
> *²Every day I will praise you*
>> *and extol your name for ever and ever.*
>
> *³Great is the LORD and most worthy of praise;*
>> *his greatness no one can fathom.*
> *⁴One generation will commend your works to another;*
>> *they will tell of your mighty acts.*
> *⁵They will speak of the glorious splendor of your majesty,*
>> *and I will meditate on your wonderful works.*
> *⁶They will tell of the power of your awesome works,*
>> *and I will proclaim your great deeds.*
> *⁷They will celebrate your abundant goodness*
>> *and joyfully sing of your righteousness.*
>
> *⁸The LORD is gracious and compassionate,*
>> *slow to anger and rich in love.*
> *⁹The LORD is good to all;*
>> *he has compassion on all he has made.*
> *¹⁰All you have made will praise you, O LORD;*
>> *your saints will extol you.*

^{11}*They will tell of the glory of your kingdom*
and speak of your might,
^{12}*so that all men may know of your mighty acts*
and the glorious splendor of your kingdom.
^{13}*Your kingdom is an everlasting kingdom,*
and your dominion endures through all generations.

*The L*ORD *is faithful to all his promises*
and loving toward all he has made.
^{14}*The L*ORD *upholds all those who fall*
and lifts up all who are bowed down.
^{15}*The eyes of all look to you,*
and you give them their food at the proper time.
^{16}*You open your hand*
and satisfy the desires of every living thing.

^{17}*The L*ORD *is righteous in all his ways*
and loving toward all he has made.
^{18}*The L*ORD *is near to all who call on him,*
to all who call on him in truth.
^{19}*He fulfills the desires of those who fear him;*
he hears their cry and saves them.
^{20}*The L*ORD *watches over all who love him,*
but all the wicked he will destroy.

^{21}*My mouth will speak in praise of the L*ORD.
Let every creature praise his holy name
for ever and ever.

—Psalm 145

2. The psalmist praises God for his "mighty acts" (verse 4). What are some of God's mighty acts that you think deserve praise?

3. How does thinking about God's mighty acts affect your view of him?

4. The psalmist says that God is "gracious and compassionate" (verse 8). How have you experienced God's compassion?

5. In verse 5 the psalmist praises "the glorious splendor of [God's] majesty." What pictures come to mind when you think of this glorious splendor?

6. The psalmist says, "The LORD is faithful to all his promises" (verse 13). What are some of God's promises that are especially important to you?

How have you experienced God's faithfulness?

7. Verses 14–20 recount things God does for us. Read through these verses and share with the group one that is especially important for you personally.

8. Even when we know that all of these things about God are true, there is still a voice inside us that says, "Yes, but. . . ." He fulfills the desires of those who fear him, *but* we all have unfulfilled desires. He watches over all who love him, *but* bad things happen even to people who love him deeply. What are the voices or experiences in your heart that press you to doubt what this psalm says about God?

9. Take some time to pray for each group member in the areas they shared in question 8. Speak God's promises into areas of their doubts or painful experiences. Pray that God would open their eyes to his faithfulness, wisdom, power, and love.

There really aren't neatly packaged answers to our doubts. The only satisfactory answer is our direct experience of God himself. When we know we've experienced his faithfulness over and over, then we can keep responding to him in faith, even when life gets confusing.

10. What are the signs of a surrendered life? The Purpose-Driven Life Health Assessment on page 72 looks at a few of them. Take a few minutes right now to rate yourself in the SURREN-DERING section of the assessment. You won't have to share your scores with the group.

11. Pair up with your spiritual partner or someone in the group with whom you feel comfortable discussing your assessment. We recommend that men partner with men and women with women. Groups of three are also fine. Talk about these three questions:

- **What's hot?** (In what ways are you doing well?)
- **What's not?** (In which areas do you need the most growth?)
- **What's next?** (What is one goal that you think God would like you to work on over the next thirty days to deepen your relationship with him? What will you do to reach that goal?)

Here are examples of possible goals:

☐ I will attend church weekly and concentrate on opening my heart to God in worship.

☐ I will take the lead (or assist) in helping this group experiment with ways to worship together.

☐ I will pray through a psalm on my own every weekday morning.

☐ I will maintain the group's prayer and praise list to keep track of answered prayers.

☐ I will read through one book of the Bible and journal on what I learn about God.

Write your goal here:

The person you've paired up with can be your spiritual partner to support you in reaching your goal. In two of the next four group sessions you will briefly check in with your spiritual partner about your personal progress. You can also call or send an E-mail to each other between meetings. It's astonishing how a little prayer and encouragement strengthens us to follow through on our plans!

If you've never taken the Purpose-Driven Life Health Assessment, consider rating yourself in the remaining four areas on your own this week.

SURRENDERING YOUR LIFE FOR GOD'S PLEASURE   20 min.

Music has an amazing power to open our hearts to God's presence. And a small group is a great setting for worshiping by means of music. Intimacy with one another increases your intimacy with God. However, many people pull back from this intimacy or are just plain embarrassed to sing. If someone in your group plays a piano or guitar, that's a huge advantage. If not, you can still worship God through music by playing one of the many CDs recorded just for this purpose. Your local Christian bookstore almost certainly carries them.

12. If you have a CD, a guitar, or a piano, play two songs. Group members can sing along, or worship in silence if they choose. Ask people to close their eyes so they won't be distracted by looking at each other. Let the music draw you into worship. Afterward you can talk about whether the group wants to do this again, and what could be done differently to make the experience even better.

As you leave, remember

- your goal for the next thirty days.
- to keep on with your daily devotions.
- to hide God's Word in your heart through your weekly Scripture memory verse.

STUDY NOTES

King ... kingdom. In our era of democracy, kings are out of fashion. We don't trust people who claim a right to rule us. We've seen power abused so often. In fact, the framers of the United States Constitution so mistrusted kings that they did everything they could to create a government in which no leader could ever amass too much power. This psalm, therefore, asserts things that go against our grain: There is someone in the universe who has the right to be called King. He has a right to rule, not because he has been elected by his citizens, but because (1) he made his citizens, and (2) he is a thoroughly trustworthy ruler. Absolute power will not corrupt him. This is the central issue we face when we consider worship and surrender: Does God deserve to be our King, or not?

☐ *For Further Study* on this topic, read Isaiah 40:28–31; 44:6–8; 1 Chronicles 29:11–12.

☐ *Weekly Memory Verse:* Psalm 145:3

☐ *The Purpose-Driven Life Reading Plan:* Day 9

NOTES

If you're using the DVD along with this curriculum, please use this space to take notes on the teaching for this session.

SURRENDERING YOUR PAST

In the twenty-eighth week of my pregnancy with triplets, I could no longer prevent the onset of early labor. I gave birth to Melody without a doctor present, but my other two babies needed a C-section. It took a half hour for the doctor to arrive to perform the operation, and during that time several things went wrong. The hospital discharged us without a word of possible problems, but within a few months it was clear that Meagan and Michelle were not okay. They had cerebral palsy because of their prematurity and the delayed C-section. The doctor said Meagan might never walk or talk, and Michelle would be affected to a lesser degree.

I felt bitter toward the doctor every day for several years. Then I joined a small group that helped me begin to make peace with my past. I knew I needed to surrender all of myself to God—my hurts and sorrows as well as my daughters' lives. I needed to begin the process of forgiveness. After many months of prayer, talking, and journaling, Brett and I made an appointment to see our doctor. I will never forget that meeting, full of memories and tears, love and tenderness. God did a work of forgiveness in our lives for which I will forever be amazed and thankful. His grace enabled us to surrender our past to him.

—Dee

CONNECTING WITH GOD'S FAMILY   10 min.

God wants us to worship him with every part of our lives, including our past. When we think about surrendering our past to God, our minds may jump immediately to painful memories. But surrendering the good things is just as important. Let's begin by looking at some of our positive memories.

1. What is one positive element of your past that has helped to shape who you are today?

GROWING TO BE LIKE CHRIST

Maybe you think your past isn't worth giving to God. Maybe you'd rather just move on. There is a time for "forgetting what is behind and straining toward what is ahead" (Philippians 3:13), but first comes a decision to *offer* to God "what is behind." All of it—good and bad. Some of us, like Dee, need to release and forgive hurts. Others, like Paul in this passage, find that the parts of our pasts we have always called "good" are the ones we most need to surrender:

> *If anyone else thinks he has reasons to put confidence in the flesh, I have more:* *⁵circumcised on the eighth day, of the people of Israel, of the tribe of Benjamin, a Hebrew of Hebrews; in regard to the law, a Pharisee;* *⁶as for zeal, persecuting the church; as for legalistic righteousness, faultless.*
>
> *⁷But whatever was to my profit I now consider loss for the sake of Christ.* *⁸What is more, I consider everything a loss compared to the surpassing greatness of knowing Christ Jesus my Lord, for whose sake I have lost all things. I consider them rubbish, that I may gain Christ* *⁹and be found in him, not having a righteousness of my own that comes from the law, but that which is through faith in Christ—the righteousness that comes from God and is by faith.* *¹⁰I want to know Christ and the power of his resurrection and the fellowship of sharing in his sufferings, becoming like him in his death,* *¹¹and so, somehow, to attain to the resurrection from the dead.*
>
> —Philippians 3:4–11

2. What do you learn about Paul's past—good and bad—from verses 4–6?

3. Paul's past made him a *somebody* in the Jewish culture of his day. How did he view that status compared to knowing and serving Christ (verses 7–8)?

4. How do you respond to Paul's attitude that his ethnic heritage is "rubbish" compared to knowing Christ? Can you imagine saying that about your heritage? Explain.

5. What did Paul want from God that made him willing to surrender his past to God?

6. Paul's past included sin—"persecuting the church" (verse 6), even to the point of aiding in the killing of Christians. What do you think is involved in surrendering such a big sin to God?

7. Paul actually *wanted* "the fellowship of sharing in [Christ's] sufferings" (verse 10). Why would someone take this view of suffering?

SURRENDERING YOUR LIFE FOR GOD'S PLEASURE   30 min.

Surrendering the past means ceasing to let the past block us from embracing God's plan for our future. It can mean giving something up, as Paul did when he turned his back on his opportunities in the Jewish community in order to be a missionary for Jesus Christ. Or it can mean letting God rule and guide us in a situation we aren't literally giving away. Dee didn't stop being the mother of special needs children when she surrendered the situation to God. Paul didn't stop being Jewish, but he did stop letting his pride in his ethnic background block him from reaching out to non-Jews. Paul— and Dee as well—allowed God to use both the good and the bad in their lives in whatever way God desired.

8. God invites you to surrender *all* of your past to him. The parts you're proud of. The hurts. The sins. Which ones are most challenging for you to surrender?

- ☐ ethnic background (Are you open to relationships outside your own ethnic group?)
- ☐ religious background (Have you let go of religious experiences that have colored your view of God?)
- ☐ social status (Can you accept a standard of living different from what you came to expect you would have as you were growing up? Or can you overcome shame about your social upbringing?)
- ☐ income (Are you willing to use your financial success to further God's kingdom, even if it means spending less on

things than you'd like to? Or can you trust and be grateful to God, even if you're not making as much money as you'd like to be making?)

- ☐ education
- ☐ work history
- ☐ marital and/or dating history
- ☐ health history
- ☐ accomplishments
- ☐ failures
- ☐ disappointments
- ☐ good deeds
- ☐ misdeeds
- ☐ hurts

9. What is a beginning step you can take to surrender one area of your past? For example, you might

- write a letter to God, thanking him for your current standard of living.
- start a conversation to get to know someone from a different ethnic group.
- write a letter to your parents (you may never send it but simply write it), forgiving them for something that happened when you were young.
- confide in someone about your dating history, and pray with this person to receive God's forgiveness.

Even if you don't feel comfortable telling the whole group about the step you plan to take, write your plan here:

10. What will this step of surrender cost you? (For example, money, time, risk in a relationship, or openness to something unfamiliar.)

11. What will you gain if you choose the path of surrender and embrace sharing in Christ's sufferings?

12. How can the group pray for you this week? Take time to pray for each other.

DEVELOPING YOUR SHAPE TO SERVE OTHERS   20 min.

13. Healthy small groups integrate all five purposes of the church deep within the heart of every member (see pages 11–14). Different members have different areas that particularly interest them. Using the gifts and interests that God has given you allows your group to grow in new and different ways. Take a moment to identify which group members would be gifted in which areas. (It's fine to let two people share a role.) Write the names of the people in the space to the left of each purpose. Also circle one or two areas you'd be open to helping out with.

_____ **CONNECTING**: Plan a social event for the group, *and/or* call unconnected or absent members each week to see how they're doing.

_____ **GROWING**: Encourage personal devotions through group discussions and spiritual (accountability) partners, *and/or* facilitate a three- or four-person discussion during your Bible study next week.

_____ **DEVELOPING**: Ensure that every member finds a group role or responsibility, *and/or* coordinate a group service project in your church or community.

_____ **SHARING**: Collect names of unchurched friends for whom the group could pray and share updates, *and/or* help launch a six-week starter group with other friends or unconnected people.

_____ **SURRENDERING**: Coordinate the group's prayer and praise list (a list of prayer requests and answers to prayer), *and/or* lead the group in a brief worship time, using a CD, video, or instrument.

STUDY NOTES

Circumcised . . . of the tribe of Benjamin, a Hebrew of Hebrews . . . a Pharisee . . . legalistic righteousness. All of these describe the perfect Jew. Circumcision was the mark of a Jewish male, and some Jewish Christians believed that non-Jews needed to be circumcised in order to be real followers of Jesus. Paul disagreed. He could trace his lineage to one of the foremost Hebrew tribes, so if pure bloodline was what mattered to Jesus, Paul had that. He belonged to the Pharisees, the most respected religious party within Judaism, so if belonging to the high-status club was what mattered to Jesus, Paul had that too. He could even claim to have followed all the rules of his religion. Paul was the equivalent of a white American who could trace his bloodline back to the *Mayflower*, who went to all the right Christian schools, and who followed all the rules of Christian culture perfectly.

Persecuting the church. Paul helped to lead the earliest efforts to stamp out the followers of Jesus. Acts 7:54–8:3 describes his participation in the murder of Stephen and the further persecution that followed. Acts 9 tells how Jesus revealed himself to Paul while Paul was in the middle of his anti-Christian crusade.

Rubbish. Paul likens his ethnic heritage and past accomplishments to a heap of garbage compared to knowing Jesus.

Knowing Christ Jesus my Lord. The kind of knowing that can only be accomplished through personal experience—through time spent together. To really know someone means you talk together about life, share common experiences, and listen to one another.

The power of his resurrection and the fellowship of sharing in his sufferings. The most vivid way Paul can describe this relationship is by describing his fellowship with Jesus in both Jesus' resurrection from the dead and the sufferings Jesus endured on the cross. Paul experienced resurrection power when Jesus Christ transformed his heart. The power of the Holy Spirit was also a key element of Paul's ministry (Acts 16:16–40, 1 Corinthians 2:4–5). He also experienced great suffering throughout his ministry, including being hungry, cold, robbed, flogged, and imprisoned (2 Corinthians 11:22–33).

☐ *For Further Study* on this topic, read John 17:3; 1 John 2:3–4, 13; 5:20.

☐ *Weekly Memory Verse:* Psalm 139:16

☐ *The Purpose-Driven Life Reading Plan:* Day 10

NOTES

If you're using the DVD along
with this curriculum, please use
this space to take notes on the
teaching for this session.

SURRENDERING YOUR FUTURE

Brett came home from a conference with the news that he wanted me to consider moving from our Southern California home to the Midwest. He wanted to do a one-year internship to learn how to plant a new church. At the time our son Josh was three, and I was seven months pregnant with our daughter Breanna. I loved our home, our church, our ministry, and our friends. But I felt I needed to consider moving, just because Brett was so excited about it. I needed to take my present, my future, and my joys and fears and set them all before God to discern his desire for my life. Over time, I concluded he did want us to take the step of faith and make the move.

The one-year internship turned into five years. I never would have planned the events that transpired. Although it was one of the most challenging seasons of my life, it was a time God used more than any other to mold me. God's path often leads through places I would not choose, but I love what he does along the way as he shows me more of himself and teaches me that I can trust him fully.

—Dee

CONNECTING WITH GOD'S FAMILY   10 min.

1. What is one thing you hope for in your future?

GROWING TO BE LIKE CHRIST

Hope is about the future. Hope is wanting and believing in something you don't have yet. And in that space between wanting and having, between the present and the future, lies a gap that you can fill with one of three things: despair, fear, or faith. Despair is the decision to quit hoping, to quit wanting anything because disappointment has broken your heart. Fear seeps in when you want something but lack confidence in God's faithfulness. Faith upholds you when you want, and even when you ache while you don't have what you want. It helps you stay focused on God's trustworthiness. The writer to the Hebrews explains it this way:

> Now faith is being sure of what we hope for and certain of what we do not see. ²This is what the ancients were commended for.
>
> ³By faith we understand that the universe was formed at God's command, so that what is seen was not made out of what was visible. . . .
>
> ⁶And without faith it is impossible to please God, because anyone who comes to him must believe that he exists and that he rewards those who earnestly seek him.
>
> ⁷By faith Noah, when warned about things not yet seen, in holy fear built an ark to save his family. By his faith he condemned the world and became heir of the righteousness that comes by faith.
>
> ⁸By faith Abraham, when called to go to a place he would later receive as his inheritance, obeyed and went, even though he did not know where he was going. ⁹By faith he made his home in the promised land like a stranger in a foreign country; he lived in tents, as did Isaac and Jacob, who were heirs with him of the same promise. ¹⁰For he was looking forward to the city with foundations, whose architect and builder is God.
>
> ¹¹By faith Abraham, even though he was past age—and Sarah herself was barren—was enabled to become a father because he considered him faithful who had made the promise. ¹²And so from this one man, and he as good as dead, came descendants as numerous as the stars in the sky and as countless as the sand on the seashore.

*13All these people were still living by faith when they died.
They did not receive the things promised; they only saw them
and welcomed them from a distance. And they admitted that
they were aliens and strangers on earth. 14People who say such
things show that they are looking for a country of their own.
15If they had been thinking of the country they had left, they
would have had opportunity to return. 16Instead, they were
longing for a better country—a heavenly one. Therefore God
is not ashamed to be called their God, for he has prepared a city
for them.*

—Hebrews 11:1–3, 6–16

2. "Faith is being . . . certain of what we do not see" (verse 1).
   What is something you're certain of that you don't see?

3. What was Noah certain of that he didn't see (verse 7)?

4. How did Noah surrender his future to God?

5. What was Abraham certain of that he didn't see (verses 8–12)?

6. How did Abraham and Sarah surrender their futures to God?

7. When Noah died, the earth was still devastated by the terrible flood that had wiped out everyone except his family. When Abraham died, the only portion of the promised land he owned was a plot big enough for his own and his wife's graves. The only evidence of the great nation that would come from him was one son. What do you think it would be like to hope for so much and live to see so little?

8. The author of Hebrews talks about "a better country" (verse 15) and "a city" (verse 16) that God's people are hoping for. What do you think he means?

9. Below are some areas of your future that God invites you to surrender. Which ones are especially relevant for you right now?

☐ your job
☐ your financial future
☐ your future health
☐ your family's health
☐ your family's choices and success in life
☐ your ministry
☐ your children
☐ your children's ambitions and passions
☐ your home
☐ your status
☐ your _____

10. How does knowing you have that "better country" in your ultimate future affect your attitude toward surrendering these issues in the nearer future?

Although there are no guarantees that we'll get what we want in this life, we can hold our hearts open to hope and surrender in these areas because we know the character of God. God is faithful.

 SURRENDERING YOUR LIFE FOR GOD'S PLEASURE   30 min.

Sometimes when we acknowledge the ways God has been faithful in the past or in the present, our muscle of faith grows stronger. Our endurance grows as we anticipate God's faithfulness in the future. Thankfulness can turn our hearts from fear to trust. Take some time to reflect on God's faithfulness in your life right now. Thank him for what he has done in your life.

11. Write down ten things for which you are thankful.

Put a check mark next to the items on your list that you're willing to share with the group. (It's okay to keep some of these private.)

12. Spend some time thanking God for his goodness. Give each person a chance to say, "Thank you, God, for. . . ." (naming certain items on his or her list).

13. How can the group pray for you this week? Remember any concerns you raised in question 9.

Take time to pray for each other. As you pray for each need, remember to thank God for the reality of his faithfulness that helps you trust him with your concerns.

14. Sit next to your spiritual partner(s). Together do one or more of the following:

- Share what you learned from your devotional time this week.
- Recite your memory verse.
- Tell how you're doing with the goal you set for yourself.

STUDY NOTES

Faith. Biblical faith is belief put into action. You can believe in anything you want, but you don't have faith in something until you act on it. Faith has to have an object. The object of our faith is God and his word. We respond by faith when we trust him at his word and step out and act in obedience.

Earnestly seek. From the Greek word *ekzēteō*, which means "to investigate or scrutinize."

Noah. See Genesis 6:1–9:29. Noah lived hundreds of miles from the nearest sizable body of water when God instructed him to build a massive ship that would be 450 feet long. The effort and expense of building the ark with Bronze-Age tools is hard to conceive. Noah did all this because he believed that he had heard God tell him to do so. Picture the response of your friends and relatives if you were to embark on such a project.

Abraham . . . Sarah. See Genesis 12:1–25:11. At the age of seventy-five, Abraham moved his household hundreds of miles to a region where he knew no one, because he believed that God had told him to do so. Sarah had to wait decades—long past menopause—to receive the baby God promised her. God promised that their descendants would one day be a great nation, owning the whole land of Canaan, but when Abraham and Sarah died, they owned only a plot large enough for their graves, and they had one childless son. Because God thinks in terms of decades and centuries when he makes promises, we will have trouble with the pathway of faith if we require instant gratification.

A city. See Revelation 21–22 for a description of the city that awaits us.

☐ *For Further Study* on this topic, read Genesis 5:2; 15:1–6; Matthew 8:5–13; 14:31.

☐ *Weekly Memory Verse:* Hebrews 11:6

☐ *The Purpose-Driven Life Reading Plan:* Days 11–12

NOTES

If you're using the DVD along with this curriculum, please use this space to take notes on the teaching for this session.

SURRENDERING
YOUR SUBSTITUTES

When I got out of seminary, I dove headfirst into ministry. I loved it. I lived for it. In fact, I lived *at* it. I had a wife and two children, and I was never home. Finally one day, Dee said to me, "Sometimes it seems like you don't even want to be here."

Her words pierced me. I went for a walk on the beach and realized that she was right. I felt I was getting needs met at church that weren't getting met at home with her and the kids, so I was avoiding being home. My soul was thirsty for life, and I was looking to my job instead of to God for the water of life. My family was paying the price.

—Brett

CONNECTING WITH GOD'S FAMILY   10 min.

1. What do you typically do when you feel frustrated or empty?

GROWING TO BE LIKE CHRIST   30–40 min.

No matter whom we say we worship, we really worship whatever we think, deep down, gives us life. The people of Israel, for example, worshiped the Lord, but they also worshiped other gods, because they didn't quite trust the Lord to provide what they

needed. The Lord sent the prophet Jeremiah to confront them about this betrayal:

> *Cross over to the coasts of Kittim and look,*
> > *send to Kedar and observe closely;*
> > *see if there has ever been anything like this:*
> [11]*Has a nation ever changed its gods?*
> > *(Yet they are not gods at all.)*
> *But my people have exchanged their Glory*
> > *for worthless idols.*
> [12]*"Be appalled at this, O heavens,*
> > *and shudder with great horror,"*
> > > > *declares the* LORD.
> [13]*"My people have committed two sins:*
> *They have forsaken me,*
> > *the spring of living water,*
> *and have dug their own cisterns,*
> > *broken cisterns that cannot hold water.*
> > > > —Jeremiah 2:10–13

2. What does it mean to call God "the spring of living water"? What does water signify?

3. How is worshiping an idol like digging your own cistern (water tank)?

4. Why would people dig their own cisterns rather than seek living water from God?

5. Why should the heavens shudder with horror when people do this?

It's often hard to discern when we are worshiping something other than God. Some clues are where we spend our time, where we spend our money, what we feel we can't live without, and where we turn when we feel frustrated or empty. We worship the thing we turn to for fulfillment.

6. Some people treat their jobs as the source of the water their souls need to survive. How can you tell when someone is treating his or her job like a cistern or idol?

7. Some people treat a relationship (a boyfriend, girlfriend, spouse, child) like the water source of their souls. How can you tell when someone is doing this?

8. In what ways is the water God gives better than the water we get from work, people, and other sources?

9. Below is a list of sources from which many people today seek the water of life. Some are more embarrassing to admit than others. Some (like food) are good things that simply need to be put in their proper place, not given up completely. Take a moment to scan the list. Is there anything here that matters more to you than it should? Is there anything you'd like to discuss with the group or with one person after the meeting?

- ☐ shopping
- ☐ the Internet
- ☐ home
- ☐ job
- ☐ fame
- ☐ a hobby
- ☐ perfectionism
- ☐ youth
- ☐ food
- ☐ alcohol
- ☐ ministry
- ☐ exercise
- ☐ fantasies

- ☐ pornography
- ☐ money (financial security)
- ☐ relationship
- ☐ family
- ☐ sports
- ☐ television
- ☐ beauty
- ☐ body
- ☐ dieting
- ☐ drugs
- ☐ power
- ☐ books

10. Give a pen and small piece of paper to each group member. On your paper write the name of one "cistern" you would like to surrender to God. No one else will read this.

SURRENDERING YOUR LIFE FOR GOD'S PLEASURE   30 min.

11. How can the group pray for you this week?

12. If you have a worship CD, play a song that expresses surrender. If not, have someone read aloud the following Scripture verses. During this time, group members will pray silently and offer to God the "cistern" they wrote down in question 10.

> Come, all you who are thirsty,
>   come to the waters;
> and you who have no money,
>   come, buy and eat!
> Come, buy wine and milk
>   without money and without cost.
> ²Why spend money on what is not bread,
>   and your labor on what does not satisfy?
> Listen, listen to me, and eat what is good,
>   and your soul will delight in the richest of fare.
> ³Give ear and come to me;
>   hear me, that your soul may live.
>   –Isaiah 55:1–3

> As the deer pants for streams of water,
>   so my soul pants for you, O God.
> ²My soul thirsts for God, for the living God.
>   When can I go and meet with God?
>   —Psalm 42:1–2

If people wish to offer prayers of surrender, they can do so. Then pray for the group's prayer requests.

DEVELOPING YOUR SHAPE TO SERVE OTHERS 15 min.

One thing small group members and leaders need to surrender to God is their group and their own particular role in the group. Sometimes that means

- letting a group end.
- letting a group change.
- letting God change you through your interaction with other group members.
- group members starting to share tasks that leaders have always done.
- committing yourself to pray for other group members.

13. If your group is going to continue, are there any tasks the leader has been doing that others might share? Are you willing to let God minister to the group in new ways through different people?

14. If your group is coming to an end or a point of change when you finish this study guide, make a plan to celebrate at your next meeting. How can you help your group celebrate? Who will provide refreshments?

Include a plan for worship as part of your final celebration. Consider sharing Communion together as a way of celebrating Jesus' surrender of his life for your sake. Also consider including music and a time of offering thanks to God for your group.

Instructions for sharing Communion in a small group are on page 78.

STUDY NOTES

Kittim . . . Kedar. Cyprus—the western coast of what is now Israel and Lebanon—and the desert of Syria. These were lands where tribal peoples worshiped the gods of their own tribes. There was a fair amount of religious borrowing throughout the region, but those cultures believed that it was fine to worship many gods. The Jews alone had the notion that there was one God who should be worshiped exclusively.

Living water. In everyday usage this expression simply meant running water as opposed to a still lake. But the Middle East had a desert and near-desert climate where every drop of water was precious. In an age when we can turn on a tap and get all the water we want, it's hard for us to relate to the idea that water is truly the water of life and that a person can die of thirst fairly quickly. In fact, gods of rain and rivers were among the most revered in the Middle East of Jeremiah's day, because people were willing to worship whomever could guarantee the water they needed to survive. The Lord claimed to be the true source of water, both for the body and the soul. Compare John 4:4–15, 7:37–39.

Broken cisterns. Without water the desert nomads would perish within days. A cistern was their lifeline. As the rain descended off a side of a mountain, it was trapped in a holding tank made of rocks and clay. A cistern that could hold no water put lives at risk. It would have been a disaster to think you were filling your cistern with water but when you drew from it, there was nothing there. This is a vivid picture of trying to get your needs met apart from God.

☐ *For Further Study on this topic, read Isaiah 42:17; 57:10–13; 1 Corinthians 6:12; 2 Peter 2:19.*

☐ *Weekly Memory Verse:* Philippians 3:7

☐ *The Purpose-Driven Life Reading Plan:* Day 13

NOTES

If you're using the DVD along
with this curriculum, please use
this space to take notes on the
teaching for this session.

When William Wilberforce gave his life to Christ in 1785, his first thought was to become a pastor. However, friends encouraged him to stay in the gritty world of British politics. He soon became a key figure in a group of reformers called the Clapham Circle and spent nearly fifty years combating social evils. Slavery was his chief passion. After years of effort, he and his comrades finally got a bill through Parliament in 1807 to abolish the British slave trade. Refusing to give up hope despite many setbacks, they achieved full freedom for all slaves in the British Empire in 1833. The bill passed mere days before Wilberforce died. He had offered his life to God to use in whatever way God chose, and God had given him a calling and a community beyond anything he could have imagined.

CONNECTING WITH GOD'S FAMILY   10 min.

1. What has been the high point of this group for you?

GROWING TO BE LIKE CHRIST   30–40 min.

Ultimately, to offer yourself as a living sacrifice to God is to say, "Here I am, Lord. My life belongs to you. Who would you like me to be?" There are costs involved, but those who have done this unanimously agree that the prize far outweighs the price.

Paul said all was rubbish compared to knowing Christ intimately. He surrendered to Christ, who asked him to spend three

59

decades taking the gospel to non-Jews throughout the Roman Empire. It was hard work, and Paul had no way of knowing the long-term impact of his labor. As an old man sitting in a Roman jail waiting to be executed, he looked back at his life. Here's how he described it:

> For I am already being poured out like a drink offering, and the time has come for my departure. [7]I have fought the good fight, I have finished the race, I have kept the faith. [8]Now there is in store for me the crown of righteousness, which the Lord, the righteous Judge, will award to me on that day—and not only to me, but also to all who have longed for his appearing.
>
> —2 Timothy 4:6–8

2. Read about drink offerings in the study notes on page 63. What does it mean to be poured out like a drink offering?

3. Paul compared his life to a fight and to a race. What do these comparisons tell you about a surrendered life?

4. For the cause of Christ, Paul had been beaten, shipwrecked, and imprisoned; he had gone hungry, thirsty, and sleepless (2 Corinthians 11:21–33). What made it all worthwhile?

5. What does fighting the good fight involve for you?

6. Verses 7–8 might be the words inscribed on Paul's tombstone or used in the eulogy at his funeral. In the eulogy at your funeral, what do you hope will be said about you?

DEVELOPING YOUR SHAPE TO SERVE OTHERS   15 min.

7. *(Optional)* Take a sheet of paper. At the top write, "Here I am, Lord. Use me." Then write words, phrases, sentences, or Scripture verses that sketch out whatever you think God wants your life to be about. Here are some ideas to spark your thinking:

> *He has showed you, O man, what is good.*
> *And what does the LORD require of you?*
> *To act justly and to love mercy*
> *and to walk humbly with your God.*
>
> —Micah 6:8

> *"Love the Lord your God with all your heart and with all your soul and with all your mind." ³⁸This is the first and greatest commandment. ³⁹And the second is like it: "Love your neighbor as yourself." ⁴⁰All the Law and the Prophets hang on these two commandments.*
>
> —Matthew 22:37–40

For the Son of Man came to seek and to save what was lost.

—Luke 19:10

To know Christ more intimately, to love others more honestly, to impact the world more significantly (key words: know, love, impact)

—Brett's mission statement

To serve God with all my heart and to love my family well (key words: serve, love)

—Someone else's mission statement

After about five minutes, share with the group what you've written. Don't worry if your thoughts are sketchy. This exercise is intended merely to get you thinking about what offering your life to God might involve.

SURRENDERING YOUR LIFE FOR GOD'S PLEASURE   30 min.

8. What's next for your group? Turn to the Purpose-Driven Group Agreement on page 67. Do you want to continue meeting together? If so, do you want to change anything in this agreement (times, dates, shared values, and so on)? Are there any things you'd like the group to do better as it moves forward? Take notes on this discussion.

9. Sit next to your spiritual partner(s) or pair up with another member. Together do one or more of the following:

   • Share what you learned from your devotional time this week.
   • Recite your memory verse.
   • Tell how you're doing with the goal you set for yourself.

10. How can the group pray for you this week?

11. Celebrate your life together in this group with a special time of worship. You can honor Jesus' surrender of his life on the cross by sharing Communion together. This is an opportunity to thank him for what he did for you and to respond by surrendering your own lives.

   Instructions for sharing Communion in a small group are on page 78.

STUDY NOTES

Drink offering. In Jewish rites, wine was poured on the altar or on the animal being sacrificed. Portions of the animal were often reserved for eating, but the wine was always completely consumed.

Crown of righteousness. A crown of victory and public honor, not royalty. It was customary for a victorious athlete to receive a crown of laurel leaves as his trophy. A modern analogy might be an Olympic gold medal. For higher honors, the crown was made of gold leaves. For believers, our reward is eternal. Rather than a physical trophy, our reward is being honored by the King of heaven for all of eternity because of our service to him in this life.

☐ *For Further Study* on this topic, read Numbers 15:1–12; Philippians 1:12–26; 2:14–18.

☐ *Weekly Memory Verse:* Psalm 31:5

☐ *The Purpose-Driven Life Reading Plan:* Day 14

NOTES

If you're using the DVD along with this curriculum, please use this space to take notes on the teaching for this session.

FREQUENTLY ASKED QUESTIONS

Who may attend the group?

Anybody you feel would benefit from it. As you begin, we encourage each attender to invite at least one other friend to join. A good time to join is in the first or second week of a new study. Share the names of your friends with the group members so that they can be praying for you.

How long will this group meet?

It's totally up to the group—once you come to the end of this six-week study. Most groups meet weekly for at least the first six weeks, but every other week can work as well. At the end of this study, each group member may decide if he or she wants to continue on for another six-week study. We encourage you to consider using the next study in this series. The series is designed to take you on a developmental journey to healthy, purpose-driven lives in thirty-six sessions. However, each guide stands on its own and may be taken in any order. You may take a break between studies if you wish.

Who is the leader?

This booklet will walk you through every step for an effective group. In addition, your group may have selected one or more discussion leaders. We strongly recommend that you rotate the job of facilitating your discussions so that everyone's gifts can emerge and develop. You can share other responsibilities as well, such as bringing refreshments or keeping up with those who miss a meeting. There's no reason why one or two people need to do everything; in fact, sharing ownership of the group will help *everyone* grow. Finally, the Bible says that when two or more are gathered in Jesus' name (which you are), he is there in your midst. Ultimately, God is your leader each step of the way.

Where do we find new members for our group?

This can be troubling, especially for new groups that have only a few people or for existing groups that lose a few people along the way. We encourage you to pray with your group and then brainstorm a list of people from work, church, your neighborhood, your children's school, family, the gym, and so forth. Then have each group member invite several of the people on their list. Another good strategy is to ask church leaders to make an announcement or to allow for a bulletin insert.

No matter how you find members, it's vital that you stay on the lookout for new people to join your group. All groups tend to go through some amount of healthy attrition—the result of moves, releasing new leaders, ministry opportunities, and so forth—and if the group gets too small, it could be at risk of shutting down. If you and your group stay open, you'll be amazed at the people God sends your way. The next person just might become a friend for life. You never know!

How do we handle the child care needs in our group?

Very carefully. Seriously, this can be a sensitive issue. We suggest that you empower the group to openly brainstorm solutions. You may try something that works for some and not for others, so you must just keep playing with the dials. One common solution is to meet in the living room or dining room with the adults and to share the cost of a baby-sitter (or two) who can be with the kids in a different part of the house. Another popular option is to use one home for the kids and a second home (close by or a phone call away) for the adults. Finally, you could rotate the responsibility of providing a lesson of some sort for the kids. This last idea can be an incredible blessing to you and the kids. We've done it, and it's worked great! Again, the best approach is to encourage the group to dialogue openly about both the problem and the solution.

PURPOSE-DRIVEN
GROUP AGREEMENT

It's a good idea for every group to put words to their shared values, expectations, and commitments. A written agreement will help you avoid unspoken agendas and disappointed expectations. You'll discuss your agreement in session 1, and then you'll revisit it in session 6 to decide whether you want to modify anything as you move forward as a group. (Alternatively, you may agree to end your group in session 6.) Feel free to modify anything that doesn't work for your group.

If the idea of having a written agreement is unfamiliar to your group, we encourage you to give it a try. A clear agreement is invaluable for resolving conflict constructively and for setting your group on a path to health.

We agree to the following values:

Clear Purpose   To grow healthy spiritual lives by building a healthy small group community. In addition, we _____
_____
_____
_____
_____

Group Attendance   To give priority to the group meeting (call if I will be late or absent)

Safe Environment   To help create a safe place where people can be heard and feel loved (please, no quick answers, snap judgments, or simple fixes)

Confidentiality   To keep anything that is shared strictly confidential and within the group

Spiritual Health   To give group members permission to help me live a healthy spiritual life that is pleasing to God (see the health assessment and health plan)

Inviting People	To keep an open chair in our group and share Jesus' dream of finding a shepherd for every sheep by inviting newcomers
Shared Ownership	To remember that every member is a minister and to encourage each attender to share a small group role or serve on one of the purpose teams (page 70)
Rotating Leaders	To encourage someone new to facilitate the group each week and to rotate homes and refreshments as well (see Small Group Calendar)
Spiritual Partners	To pair up with one other group member whom I can support more diligently and help to grow spiritually (my spiritual partner is _____)

We agree to the following expectations:

• Refreshments/Mealtimes _____

• Child care _____

• When we will meet (day of week) _____

• Where we will meet (place) _____

• We will begin at (time)_____ and end at _____

• We will do our best to have some or all of us attend a worship service together. Our primary worship service time will be _____

• Review date of this agreement: _____

We agree to the following commitment:

Father, to the best of my ability, in light of what I know to be true, I commit the next season of my life to CONNECTING with your family, GROWING to be more like Christ, DEVELOPING my shape for ministry, SHARING my life mission every day, and SURRENDERING my life for your pleasure.

_____	_____	_____
Name	Date	Spiritual Partner (witness)

SMALL GROUP CALENDAR

Healthy purpose-driven groups share responsibilities and group ownership. This usually doesn't happen overnight but progressively over time. Sharing responsibilities and ownership ensures that no one person carries the group alone. The calendar below can help you in this area. You can also add a social event, mission project, birthdays, or days off to your calendar. This should be completed after your first or second meeting. Planning ahead will facilitate better attendance and greater involvement from others.

Date	Lesson	Location	Dessert/Meal	Facilitator
Monday, January 15	1	Steve and Laura's	Joe	Bill

APPENDIX

PURPOSE TEAM ROLES

The Bible makes clear that every member, not just the small group leader, is a minister in the body of Christ. In a purpose-driven small group (just like in a purpose-driven church), every member plays a role on the team. Review the team roles and responsibilities below and have each member volunteer for a role, or have the group suggest a role for each member. It's best to have one or two people on each team, so you have each purpose covered. Serving in even a small capacity will not only help your leader grow but will also make the group more fun for everyone. Don't hold back. Join a team!

The opportunities below are broken down by the five purposes and then by a *crawl* (beginning group role), *walk* (intermediate group role), or *run* (advanced group role). Try to cover the crawl and walk phases if you can.

Purpose Team Roles		Purpose Team Members
Fellowship Team (**CONNECTING** with God's Family)		
Crawl:	Host social events or group activities	____________
Walk:	Serve as a small group inviter	____________
Run:	Lead the CONNECTING time each week	____________
Discipleship Team (**GROWING** to Be Like Christ)		
Crawl:	Ensure that each member has a simple plan and a partner for personal devotions	____________
Walk:	Disciple a few younger group members	____________
Run:	Facilitate the Purpose-Driven Life Health Assessment and Purpose-Driven Life Health Plan processes	____________

Ministry Team (**DEVELOPING** Your Shape for Ministry)

Crawl: Ensure that each member finds a group role _____
or a purpose team responsibility

Walk: Plan a ministry project for the group in the _____
church or community

Run: Help each member discover and develop _____
a SHAPE-based ministry in the church

Evangelism (Missions) Team (**SHARING** Your Life Mission Every Day)

Crawl: Coordinate the group prayer and praise list _____
of non-Christian friends and family members

Walk: Pray for group mission opportunities and _____
plan a group cross-cultural adventure

Run: Plan as a group to attend a holiday service, _____
host a neighborhood party, or create a seeker
event for your non-Christian friends

Worship Team (**SURRENDERING** Your Life for God's Pleasure)

Crawl: Maintain the weekly group prayer and praise _____
list or journal

Walk: Lead a brief worship time in your group _____
(CD/video/a cappella)

Run: Plan a Communion time, prayer walk, foot _____
washing, or an outdoor worship experience

PURPOSE-DRIVEN LIFE HEALTH ASSESSMENT

	Just Beginning	Getting Going	Well Developed

CONNECTING WITH GOD'S FAMILY

I am deepening my understanding of and friendship with God in community with others — 1 2 3 4 5

I am growing in my ability both to share and to show my love to others — 1 2 3 4 5

I am willing to share my real needs for prayer and support from others — 1 2 3 4 5

I am resolving conflict constructively and am willing to forgive others — 1 2 3 4 5

CONNECTING Total _____

GROWING TO BE LIKE CHRIST

I have a growing relationship with God through regular time in the Bible and in prayer (spiritual habits) — 1 2 3 4 5

I am experiencing more of the characteristics of Jesus Christ (love, joy, peace, patience, kindness, self-control, etc.) in my life — 1 2 3 4 5

I am avoiding addictive behaviors (food, television, busyness, and the like) to meet my needs — 1 2 3 4 5

I am spending time with a Christian friend (spiritual partner) who celebrates and challenges my spiritual growth — 1 2 3 4 5

GROWING Total _____

DEVELOPING YOUR SHAPE TO SERVE OTHERS

I have discovered and am further developing my unique God-given shape for ministry — 1 2 3 4 5

I am regularly praying for God to show me opportunities to serve him and others — 1 2 3 4 5

I am serving in a regular (once a month or more) ministry in the church or community — 1 2 3 4 5

I am a team player in my small group by sharing some group role or responsibility — 1 2 3 4 5

DEVELOPING Total _____

SHARING YOUR LIFE MISSION EVERY DAY

I am cultivating relationships with non-Christians and praying
for God to give me natural opportunities to share his love   1 2 3 4 5

I am investing my time in another person or group who needs
to know Christ personally   1 2 3 4 5

I am regularly inviting unchurched or unconnected friends to
my church or small group   1 2 3 4 5

I am praying and learning about where God can use me and
our group cross-culturally for missions   1 2 3 4 5

SHARING Total _____

SURRENDERING YOUR LIFE FOR GOD'S PLEASURE

I am experiencing more of the presence and power of God in
my everyday life   1 2 3 4 5

I am faithfully attending my small group and weekend services
to worship God   1 2 3 4 5

I am seeking to please God by surrendering every area of my life
(health, decisions, finances, relationships, future, etc.) to him   1 2 3 4 5

I am accepting the things I cannot change and becoming
increasingly grateful for the life I've been given   1 2 3 4 5

SURRENDERING Total_____

Total your scores for each purpose, and place them on the chart below. Reassess
your progress at the end of thirty days. Be sure to select your spiritual partner and
the one area in which you'd like to make progress over the next thirty days.

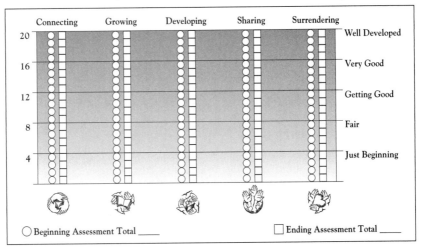

PURPOSE-DRIVEN LIFE HEALTH PLAN

My Name _____ Date _____

My Spiritual Partner _____ Date _____

Possibilities

Plan
(make one goal for each area)

CONNECTING WITH GOD'S FAMILY
Hebrews 10:24–25; Ephesians 2:19
How can I deepen my relationships with others?

- Attend my group more faithfully

- Schedule lunch with a group member

- Begin praying for a spiritual mentor

WHO is/are my shepherd(s)?

NAME: _____

GROWING TO BE LIKE CHRIST
Colossians 1:28; Ephesians 4:15
How can I grow to be like Christ?

- Commit to personal time with God three days a week

- Ask a friend for devotional accountability

- Begin journaling my prayers

WHAT is my Spiritual Health Plan?

RENEWAL DATE: _____

DEVELOPING YOUR SHAPE TO SERVE OTHERS

Ephesians 4:11–13; 1 Corinthians 12:7; 1 Peter 3:10

How can I develop my shape for ministry?

- Begin praying for a personal ministry

- Attend a gift discovery class

- Serve together at a church event or in the community

WHERE am I serving others?

MINISTRY: _____

SHARING YOUR LIFE MISSION EVERY DAY

Matthew 28:18–20; Acts 20:24

How can I share my faith every day?

- Start meeting for lunch with a seeker friend

- Invite a non-Christian relative to church

- Pray for and support an overseas missionary

WHEN am I sharing my life mission?

TIME: _____

SURRENDERING YOUR LIFE FOR GOD'S PLEASURE

How can I surrender my life for God's pleasure?

- Submit one area to God

- Be honest about my struggle and hurt

- Buy a music CD for worship in my car and in the group

HOW am I surrendering my life today?

AREA: _____

	Progress (renew and revise)	Progress (renew and revise)	Progress (renew and revise)
	30 days/Date _____ ☐ ☐ ☐ ☐ Weekly check-in with my spiritual partner or group	60-90 days/Date _____ ☐ ☐ ☐ ☐ Weekly check-in with my spiritual partner or group	120+ days/Date _____ ☐ ☐ ☐ ☐ Weekly check-in with my spiritual partner or group
CONNECTING			
GROWING			
DEVELOPING			
SHARING			
SURRENDERING			

SPIRITUAL PARTNERS'
CHECK-IN PAGE

My Name _____ Spiritual Partner's Name _____

	Our Plans	Our Progress
Week 1		
Week 2		
Week 3		
Week 4		
Week 5		
Week 6		

Briefly check in each week and write down your personal plans and progress for the next week (or even for the next few weeks). This could be done (before or after the meeting) on the phone, through an E-mail message, or even in person from time to time.

SERVING COMMUNION

Churches vary in their treatment of Communion (the Lord's Supper). Here is one simple form by which a small group can share this experience. You can adapt this form as necessary, depending on your church's beliefs.

Steps in Serving Communion

1. Out of the context of your own experience, say something brief about God's love, forgiveness, grace, mercy, commitment, tenderheartedness, or faithfulness. Connect your words with the personal stories of the group. For example, "These past few weeks I've experienced God's mercy in the way he untangled the situation with my son. And I've seen God show mercy to others of us here too, especially to Jean and Roger." If you prefer, you can write down ahead of time what you want to say.

2. Read 1 Corinthians 11:23–26:

   The Lord Jesus, on the night he was betrayed, took bread, [24]and when he had given thanks, he broke it and said, "This is my body, which is for you; do this in remembrance of me." [25]In the same way, after supper he took the cup, saying, "This cup is the new covenant in my blood; do this, whenever you drink it, in remembrance of me." [26]For whenever you eat this bread and drink this cup, you proclaim the Lord's death until he comes.

3. Pray silently and pass the bread around the circle. While the bread is being passed, you may want to reflect quietly, sing a simple praise song, or listen to a worship tape.

4. When everyone has received the bread, remind them that this represents Jesus' broken body on their behalf. Simply state, "Jesus said, 'Do this in remembrance of me.' Let us eat together," and eat the bread as a group.

5. Pray silently and serve the cup. You may pass a small tray, serve people individually, or have them pick up a cup from the table.

6. When everyone has been served, remind them that the cup represents Jesus' blood shed for them. Simply state, "The cup of the new covenant is Jesus Christ's blood shed for you. Jesus said, 'Do this in remembrance of me.' Let us drink together." Then drink the juice as a group.

7. Conclude by singing a simple song, listening to a praise song, or having a time of prayer in thanks to God.

Practical Tips in Serving Communion

1. Prepare the elements simply, sacredly, and symbolically.

2. Be sensitive to timing in your meeting.

3. Break up pieces of cracker or soft bread on a small plate or tray. *Don't* use large servings of bread or grape juice. We encourage you to use grape juice, not wine, because wine is a cause of stumbling for some people.

4. Have all of the elements prepared beforehand, and just bring them into the room or to the table when you are ready.

☐ **For Further Study**
Other Communion passages: Matthew 26:26–29; Mark 14:22–25; Luke 22:14–20; 1 Corinthians 10:16–21; 11:17–34

MEMORY VERSES

One of the most effective ways to instill biblical truth deep into our lives is to memorize key Scriptures. For many, memorization is a new concept—or perhaps one we found difficult in the past. We encourage you to stretch yourself and try to memorize these six verses.

A good way to memorize a verse is to copy it on a sheet of paper five times. Most people learn something by heart when they do this. It's also helpful to post the verse someplace where you will see it several times a day.

WEEK ONE

"Therefore, I urge you, brothers, in view of God's mercy, to offer your bodies as living sacrifices, holy and pleasing to God—this is your spiritual act of worship."

Romans 12:1

WEEK TWO

"Great is the LORD and most worthy of praise;
his greatness no one can fathom."

Psalm 145:3

WEEK THREE

"All the days ordained for me were written in your book before one of them came to be."

Psalm 139:16

WEEK FOUR

"Without faith it is impossible to please God, because anyone who comes to him must believe that he exists and that he rewards those who earnestly seek him."

Hebrew 11:6

WEEK FIVE

"But whatever was to my profit I now consider loss for the sake of Christ."

Philippians 3:7

WEEK SIX

"Into your hands I commit my spirit; redeem me, O LORD, the God of truth."

Psalm 31:5

DAILY DEVOTIONAL READINGS

We've experienced so much life change as a result of reading the Bible daily. Hundreds of people have gone through DOING LIFE TOGETHER, and they tell us that the number-one contributor to their growth was the deeper walk with God that came as a result of the daily devotions. We strongly encourage you to have everyone set a realistic goal for the six weeks. Pair people into same-gender spiritual (accountability) partners. This will improve your results tenfold. Then we encourage everyone to take a few minutes each day to **READ** the verse for the day, **REFLECT** on what God is saying to you through the verse, and **RESPOND** to God in prayer in a personal journal. Each of these verses was selected to align with the week's study. After you complete the reading, simply put a check mark in the box next to the verse. Enjoy the journey!

WEEK ONE
- ☐ Psalm 29
- ☐ Psalm 96:1–9
- ☐ Psalm 95
- ☐ Isaiah 29:13–14
- ☐ Matthew 15:8–9

WEEK TWO
- ☐ Psalm 100
- ☐ Psalm 46:10
- ☐ Psalm 150
- ☐ Matthew 4:9–10
- ☐ Hebrews 13:15

WEEK THREE
- ☐ Isaiah 64:8
- ☐ Isaiah 43:18–19
- ☐ Romans 6:13
- ☐ John 4:23–24
- ☐ 1 Corinthians 10:14–22

WEEK FOUR
- ☐ Jeremiah 29:11
- ☐ Proverbs 19:21
- ☐ Psalm 16:11
- ☐ Proverbs 3:5–6
- ☐ 1 Corinthians 2:9

WEEK FIVE
- ☐ Matthew 5:6
- ☐ Matthew 6:19–24
- ☐ Matthew 6:33
- ☐ Matthew 22:37–39
- ☐ John 6:35

WEEK SIX
- ☐ Colossians 1:10–12
- ☐ Psalm 103:1–5
- ☐ Romans 12:1–2
- ☐ 2 Chronicles 16:9
- ☐ 2 Corinthians 3:18

PRAYER AND PRAISE REPORT

Briefly share your prayer requests with the large group, making notations below. Then gather in small groups of two, three, or four to pray for each need.

	Prayer Request	Praise Report
Week 1		
Week 2		
Week 3		

	Prayer Request	Praise Report
Week 4		
Week 5		
Week 6		

SAMPLE JOURNAL PAGE

Today's Passage: _____

Reflections from my HEART:

I *Honor* who you are. (Praise God for something.)

I *Express* who I'm not. (Confess any known sin.)

I *Affirm* who I am in you. (How does God see you?)

I *Request* your will for me. (Ask God for something.)

I *Thank* you for what you've done. (Thank him for something.)

Today's Action Step:

LEADERSHIP TRAINING

Small Group Leadership 101 (Top Ten Ideas for New Facilitators)

Congratulations! You have responded to the call to help shepherd Jesus' flock. There are few other tasks in the family of God that surpass the contribution you will be making. As you prepare to lead—whether it is one session or the entire series—here are a few thoughts to keep in mind. We encourage you to read these and review them with each new discussion leader before he or she leads.

1. **Remember that you are not alone.** God knows everything about you, and he knew that you would be asked to lead your group. Even though you may not feel ready to lead, this is common for all good leaders. Moses, Solomon, Jeremiah, or Timothy—they *all* were reluctant to lead. God promises, "Never will I leave you; never will I forsake you" (Hebrews 13:5). Whether you are leading for one evening, for several weeks, or for a lifetime, you will be blessed as you serve.

2. **Don't try to do it alone.** Pray right now for God to help you build a healthy leadership team. If you can enlist a coleader to help you lead the group, you will find your experience to be much richer. This is your chance to involve as many people as you can in building a healthy group. All you have to do is call and ask people to help—you'll be surprised at the response.

3. **Just be yourself.** If you won't be you, who will? God wants to use your unique gifts and temperament. Don't try to do things exactly like another leader; do them in a way that fits you! Just admit it when you don't have an answer and apologize when you make a mistake. Your group will love you for it!—and you'll sleep better at night.

4. **Prepare for your meeting ahead of time.** Review the session and the leader's notes, and write down your responses to each question. Pay special attention to exercises that ask group members to do something other than engage in discussion. These exercises will help your group *live* what the Bible teaches, not just talk about it. Be sure you understand how an exercise works, and bring any necessary supplies (such as paper or pens) to your meeting. If the exercise employs one of the items in the appendix (such as the Purpose-Driven Life Health Assessment), be sure to look over that item so

you'll know how it works. Finally, review "Read Me First" on pages 11–14 so you'll remember the purpose of each section in the study.

5. **Pray for your group members by name.** Before you begin your session, go around the room in your mind and pray for each member by name. You may want to review the prayer list at least once a week. Ask God to use your time together to touch the heart of every person uniquely. Expect God to lead you to whomever he wants you to encourage or challenge in a special way. If you listen, God will surely lead!

6. **When you ask a question, be patient.** Someone will eventually respond. Sometimes people need a moment or two of silence to think about the question, and if silence doesn't bother you, it won't bother anyone else. After someone responds, affirm the response with a simple "thanks" or "good job." Then ask, "How about somebody else?" or "Would someone who hasn't shared like to add anything?" Be sensitive to new people or reluctant members who aren't ready to say, pray, or do anything. If you give them a safe setting, they will blossom over time.

7. **Provide transitions between questions.** When guiding the discussion, always read aloud the transitional paragraphs and the questions. Ask the group if anyone would like to read the paragraph or Bible passage. Don't call on anyone, but ask for a volunteer, and then be patient until someone begins. Be sure to thank the person who reads aloud.

8. **Break up into small groups each week, or they won't stay.** If your group has more than seven people, we strongly encourage you to have the group gather in discussion circles of three or four people during the GROWING or SURRENDERING sections of the study. With a greater opportunity to talk in a small circle, people will connect more with the study, apply more quickly what they're learning, and ultimately get more out of it. A small circle also encourages a quiet person to participate and tends to minimize the effects of a more vocal or dominant member. And it can help people feel more loved in your group. When you gather again at the end of the section, you can have one person summarize the highlights from each circle.

Small circles are also helpful during prayer time. People who are unaccustomed to praying aloud will feel more comfortable trying it with just two or three others. Also, prayer requests won't take as much time, so circles will have more time to actually pray. When you gather back with the whole group, you can have one person from each circle briefly update everyone on the prayer requests. People are more willing to pray in small circles if they know that the whole group will hear all the prayer requests.

9. **Rotate facilitators weekly.** At the end of each meeting, ask the group who should lead the following week. Let the group help select your weekly facilitator. You may be perfectly capable of leading each time, but you will help others grow in their faith and gifts if you give them opportunities to lead. You can use the Small Group Calendar on page 69 to fill in the names of all six meeting leaders at once if you prefer.

10. **One final challenge (for new or first-time leaders): Before your first opportunity to lead, look up each of the five passages listed below.** Read each one as a devotional exercise to help prepare yourself with a shepherd's heart. Trust us on this one. If you do this, you will be more than ready for your first meeting.

- ☐ Matthew 9:36
- ☐ 1 Peter 5:2-4
- ☐ Psalm 23
- ☐ Ezekiel 34:11–16
- ☐ 1 Thessalonians 2:7–8, 11–12

Small Group Leadership Lifters (Weekly Leadership Tips)

And David shepherded them with integrity of heart;
with skillful hands he led them.

Psalm 78:73

David provides a model of a leader who has a heart for God, a desire to shepherd God's people, and a willingness to develop the skills of a leader. The following is a series of practical tips for new and existing small group leaders. These principles and practices have proved to cultivate healthy, balanced groups in over a thousand examples.

1. Don't Leave Home without It: A Leader's Prayer

"The prayer of a righteous man [or woman] is powerful and effective" (James 5:16). From the very beginning of this study, why not commit to a simple prayer of renewal in your heart and in the hearts of your members? Take a moment right now and write a simple prayer as you begin:

Father, help me _____

_____

_____

2. Pay It Now or Pay It Later: Group Conflict

Most leaders and groups avoid conflict, but healthy groups are willing to do what it takes to learn and grow through conflict. Much group conflict can be avoided if the leader lets the group openly discuss and decide its direction, using the Purpose-Driven Group Agreement. Healthy groups are alive. Conflict is a sign of maturity, not mistakes. Sometimes you may need to get outside counsel, but don't be afraid. See conflict as an opportunity to grow, and always confront it so it doesn't create a cancer that can kill the group over time (Matthew 18:15–20).

3. Lead from Weakness

The apostle Paul said that God's power was made perfect in Paul's weakness (2 Corinthians 12:9). This is clearly the opposite of what most leaders think, but it provides the most significant model of humility, authority, and spiritual power. It was Jesus' way at the cross. So share your struggles along with your successes, confess your sins to one another along with your celebrations, and ask for prayer for yourself along with praying for others. God will be pleased, and your group will grow deeper. If you humble yourself under God's mighty hand, he will exalt you at the proper time (Matthew 23:12).

4. What Makes Jesus Cry: A Leader's Focus

In Matthew 9:35–38, Jesus looked at the crowds following him and saw them as sheep without a shepherd. He was moved with compassion, because they were "distressed and downcast" (NASB); the NIV says they were "harassed and helpless." The Greek text implies that he was moved to the point of tears.

Never forget that you were once one of those sheep yourself. We urge you to keep yourself and your group focused not just inwardly to each other but also outwardly to people beyond your group. Jesus said, "Follow me . . . and I will make you fishers of men" (Matthew 4:19). We assume that you and your group are following him. So how is your fishing going? As leader, you can ignite in your group Jesus' compassion for outsiders. For his sake, keep the fire burning!

5. Prayer Triplets

Prayer triplets can provide a rich blessing to you and many others. At the beginning or end of your group meeting, you can gather people into prayer triplets to share and pray about three non-Christian friends. This single strategy will increase your group's evangelistic effectiveness considerably. Be sure to get an update on the plans and progress from each of the circles. You need only ten minutes at every other meeting—but do this at least once a month. At first, some of your members may feel overwhelmed at the thought of praying for non-Christians. We've been there! But you can be confident that over time they will be renewed in their heart for lost people and experience the blessing of giving birth to triplets.

6. Race against the Clock

When your group grows in size or your members begin to feel more comfortable talking, you will inevitably feel as though you're racing against the clock. You may know the feeling very well. The good news is that there are several simple things that can help your group stick to your agreed schedule:

- The time crunch is actually a sign of relational and spiritual health, so pat yourselves on the back.
- Check in with the group to problem-solve, because they feel the tension as well.

- You could begin your meeting a little early or ask for a later ending time.
- If you split up weekly into circles of three to four people for discussion, you will double the amount of time any one person can share.
- Appoint a timekeeper to keep the group on schedule.
- Remind everyone to give brief answers.
- Be selective in the number of questions you try to discuss.
- Finally, planning the time breaks in your booklet before the group meeting begins can really keep you on track.

7. All for One and One for All: Building a Leadership Team

The statement "Together Everybody Accomplishes More" (TEAM) is especially true in small groups. The Bible clearly teaches that every member is a minister. Be sure to empower the group to share weekly facilitation, as well as other responsibilities, and seek to move every player onto a team over time. Don't wait for people to ask, because it just won't happen. From the outset of your group, try to get everybody involved. The best way to get people in the game is to have the group suggest who would serve best on what team and in what role. See Purpose Team Roles on pages 70–71 for several practical suggestions. You could also talk to people individually or ask for volunteers in the group, but don't miss this opportunity to develop every group member and build a healthy and balanced group over time.

8. Purpose-Driven Groups Produce Purpose-Driven Lives:
A Leader's Goal

As you undertake this new curriculum, especially if this is your first time as a leader, make sure you begin with the end in mind. You may have heard the phrase, "If you aim at nothing, you'll hit it every time." It's vital for your group members to review their spiritual health by using the Purpose-Driven Life Health Assessment and Purpose-Driven Life Health Plan (pages 72–76). You'll do part of the health assessment in your group in session 2 and share your results with spiritual partners for support and accountability. Each member will also set one goal for thirty days. The goal will be tied to the purpose you are studying in this particular guide. We strongly encourage you to go even further and do the entire health assessment together. Then during another group session (or on their own), members can set a goal for each of the other four purposes.

Pairing up with spiritual partners will offer invaluable support for that area of personal growth. Encourage partners to pray for one another in the area of their goals. Have partners gather at least three times during the series to share their progress and plans. This will give you and the group the best results. In order for people to follow through with their goals, you'll need to lead with vision and modeling. Share your goals with the group, and update them on how the steps you're taking have been affecting your spiritual life. If you share your progress and plans, others will follow in your footsteps.

9. Discover the Power of Pairs

The best resolutions get swept aside by busyness and forgetfulness, which is why it's important for group members to have support as they pursue a spiritual goal. Have them pair up with spiritual partners in session 2, or encourage them to seek out a Christian coworker or personal mentor. You can promise that they'll never be the same if they simply commit to supporting each other with prayer and encouragement on a weekly basis.

It's best to start with one goal in an area of greatest need. Most of the time the area will be either evangelism or consistent time with the Father in prayer and in Scripture reading. Cultivating time with God is the place to start; if group members are already doing this, they can move on to a second and third area of growth.

You just need a few victories in the beginning. Have spiritual partners check in together at the beginning or end of each group meeting. Ask them to support those check-ins with phone calls, coffee times, and E-mail messages during the week. Trust us on this one—you will see people grow like never before.

10. Don't Lose Heart: A Leader's Vision

You are a strategic player in the heavenly realm. Helping a few others grow in Christ could put you squarely in the sights of Satan himself. First Corinthians 15:58 (NASB) says, "Be steadfast, immovable, always abounding in the work of the Lord." Leading a group is not always going to be easy. Here are the keys to longevity and lasting joy as a leader:

- Be sure to refuel your soul as you give of yourself to others. We recommend that you ask a person to meet with you for personal coaching and encouragement. When asked (over coffee or lunch) to support someone in leadership, nine out of ten people say, "I'd love to!" So why not ask?
- Delegate responsibilities after the first meeting. Doing so will help group members grow, and it will give you a break as well.

- Most important, cultivating your own walk with God puts you on the offensive against Satan and increases the joy zone for everyone in your life. Make a renewed decision right now to make this happen. Don't give Satan a foothold in your heart; there is simply too much at stake.

Goals of the Session

- To understand that worship is offering your very selves to God
- To experience group worship through the psalms

Before you meet for the first time, invite as many people as you would enjoy hanging out with. It just makes the group a whole lot more fun for you as the leader. Also, ask one or two people if they'd be willing to colead with you so you don't have to do it alone.

Open your meeting with a brief prayer.

Question 1. As leader, you should be the first to answer this question. Your answer will model the amount of vulnerability you want others to imitate. If your answer is superficial, you'll set a superficial tone—but if you tell something substantive and personal, others will know that your group is a safe place to tell the truth about themselves. You might want to think about your answer ahead of time.

Be sure to give each person a chance to respond to this question, because it's an opportunity for group members to get to know each other. It's not necessary to go around the circle in order. Be aware that people may have had very different amounts of experience with worship and very different tastes in the kind of worship that is meaningful to them.

Introduction to the Series. If this is your first study guide in the DOING LIFE TOGETHER series, you'll need to take time after question 1 to orient the group to one principle that undergirds the series: *A healthy purpose-driven small group balances the five purposes of the church in order to help people balance them in their lives.* Most small groups emphasize Bible study, fellowship, and prayer. But God has called us to reach out to others as well. If the five purposes are new to your group, be sure to review the Read Me First section with your new group. In addition, the Frequently Asked Questions section could help your group understand some of the purpose-driven group basics.

Question 2. If your group has done another study guide in the DOING LIFE TOGETHER series within the past six months, you may not need to go over the Purpose-Driven Group Agreement again. It's a good idea to remind people of the agreement from time to time, but for an established group, recommitting every six months is reasonable. If you're new to the series and if you don't already have a group agreement, turn to page 67 and take about ten minutes to look at the Purpose-Driven Group Agreement. Read each value aloud in turn, and let group members comment at the end. Emphasize confidentiality—a commitment that is essential to the ability to trust each other.

"Spiritual Health" says that group members give permission to encourage each other to set spiritual goals *for themselves*. As the study progresses, a group member may set a goal to do daily devotions, or a dad may set a goal to spend half an hour each evening with his children. No one will set goals for someone else; each person will be free to set his or her own goals.

"Shared Ownership" points toward session 3, when members will be asked to help with some responsibility in the group. It may be as simple as bringing refreshments or keeping track of prayer requests. Ultimately, it's healthy for groups to rotate leadership among several, or perhaps even all, members. People grow when they contribute. However, no one should feel pressured into a responsibility.

Regarding expectations: It's amazing how many groups never take the time to make explicit plans about refreshments, child care, and other such issues. Child care is a big issue in many groups. It's important to treat it as an issue that the group as a whole needs to solve, even if the group decides that each member will make arrangements separately.

If you feel that your group needs to move on, you can save the conversation about expectations until the end of your meeting.

Question 3. Have someone read the Bible passage aloud. It's a good idea to ask someone ahead of time, because not everyone is comfortable reading aloud in public. When the passage has been read, ask question 3. Don't be afraid to allow silence while people think. It's completely normal to have periods of silence in a Bible study. You might count to seven silently. If nobody says anything, say something humorous like, "I can wait longer than you can!" It's not necessary that everyone respond to every one of the Bible study questions.

The study notes offer a definition of *mercy*, but it will be most helpful if group members can put the definition into their own words. If you get short, obvious answers to the second part of the question ("God has shown me mercy by sending Jesus to die for me"), ask the group to expand on this— How was this an act of mercy to you personally? Sometimes people know the right answers, but the right answers don't grip them. It doesn't seem real that they deserve much worse than what they have or what they're getting. If you sense that your group is blasé about God's mercy, you might share how you have experienced God's mercy for your sins.

Question 4. Help your group bridge the cultural gap to a time when animal sacrifice was part of daily life. Paul really does want his readers to picture themselves climbing onto a big stone altar and giving God permission to kill them or to live through them—whichever will best serve his purposes. This blank check would be outrageous to write except for the fact that Jesus already did it. Paul, too, allowed God to live through him for many years and eventually to lead him to martyrdom. This is drastic business.

Question 5. Again, Paul doesn't want us to superspiritualize the Christian life. He wants us to give God authority over everything we are and everything we do with our physical bodies.

Question 9. Church worship is an opportunity to acknowledge publicly that God is so merciful and magnificent that he deserves this kind of total surrender. It's an occasion to gather with others and celebrate God—and be drawn deeper into life together with God and his people. It's one of the activities that nourishes us for the daily worship of offering our bodies as living sacrifices and being transformed by the Holy Spirit.

Question 10. Try to set aside extra time throughout this study for your group to experiment with ways to worship together. Worship fuels surrender. Worship is a facet of surrender. Don't worry if you feel awkward as you try certain things. Everyone is learning together.

Question 11. The devotional passages on page 81 give your group a chance to test-drive the spiritual discipline of spending daily time with God. Encourage everyone to give it a try. There are five short readings for each session, so people can read one a day and even skip a couple of days a week. Talk to your group about committing to reading and reflecting on these verses each day. This practice has revolutionized the spiritual lives of others who have used this study, so we highly recommend it. There will be an opportunity in future sessions to share what you have discovered in your devotional reading. Remind group members of the sample journal page on page 84.

Beginning in session 2, people will have an opportunity to check in with one other member at the end of several of the group sessions to share what they learned from the Lord in their devotional time.

Consider giving one or more group members the chance to be a facilitator for a meeting. Healthy groups rotate their leadership each week. No one person has to carry all the responsibility. What's more, it helps develop everyone's gifts in a safe environment, and, best of all, you learn different things through the eyes of different people with different styles. You can use the Small Group Calendar (page 69) to help manage your rotating schedule.

Question 12. You are the expert about your group. If your members are seasoned veterans in group prayer, let them go for it. But if you have members who are new believers, new to small groups, or just new to praying aloud, suggest an option that will feel comfortable for them. Newcomers won't come back if they find themselves in the scary position of having to pray aloud as "perfectly" as the veterans. Talking to God is more significant than talking to your nation's president or to a movie star—so it's no wonder people feel intimidated! A silent prayer, a one-sentence prayer, or even a one-word prayer are completely acceptable first steps. Make sure the circles understand this so that no one feels he or she is being put on the spot.

Goals of the Session

- To become more deeply convinced of God's greatness
- To receive prayer from the group in the area of your doubts

New rotating leaders may want to meet ahead of time with an experienced leader to review the plan for the meeting. You may want to have some extra booklets on hand for any new group members.

Question 1. This is a lighthearted way to unearth people's genuine doubts about how God runs the universe. If you were God, would you clear up poverty? Give power to leaders who would make more ethical choices? Heal the sick child or the young mother who has cancer? Reveal your Son to the whole world so that everyone would worship him?

Question 2. Chief on this list would be the birth, life, death, and resurrection of God's Son, Jesus Christ. The Bible is full of many other mighty acts that would be worth listing.

Questions 4, 6. It's important for people to tell stories of how they have experienced God's good qualities. Hearing others' stories bolsters those who are waiting to see God's faithfulness or questioning his compassion.

Question 8. Some groups may be reluctant to admit that there are any clouds to darken their perfect view of God. If your group seems to think it's not okay to admit this, you may need to go first. What is one of your unfulfilled desires? Having an unfulfilled desire doesn't mean that you lack faith or contentment. It simply means that you don't live in paradise and God isn't the great Santa in the sky. Our fallen world presents much evidence that seems to conflict with what this psalm asserts, and God will not be threatened if you put it on the table.

Question 9. This is extremely important. If God seems to be touching people as you pray for them, you may decide to shorten one of the later sections of the study. You can save the Personal Health Assessment (question 10) for your next session if necessary.

Question 10. Familiarize yourself with the Purpose-Driven Life Health Assessment before the meeting. You may want to take the assessment yourself ahead of time and think about your goal. Then you can give group members a real-life example of what you are actually committed to doing. We also encourage you to complete a simple goal under each purpose. Ask your coleader or a trusted friend to review it with you. Then you'll understand the power of this tool and the support you can gain from a spiritual partner.

Offer the health assessment in a spirit of grace. It should make people hungry to see the Holy Spirit work in their lives, not ashamed that they're falling short. Nobody can do these things in the power of the flesh! And sometimes the most mature believers have the clearest perception of the areas in which they need considerable help from the Spirit.

Question 11. Help guide people to pair up with partners with whom they will have a good chemistry. Spiritual partnership works best when people trust each other. Point out the Spiritual Partners' Check-In Page on page 79, which can give partners a structure for checking in with each other. Bear in mind that some personalities love self-assessments and setting goals, while others are more resistant. Some people who routinely set goals at work may be taken aback at the idea of setting a goal for their spiritual lives. Assure everyone that their goals can be small steps, that no one will be pressured into performing or humiliated for falling short, and that God is always eager to give grace.

The Purpose-Driven Life Health Plan on pages 74–76 is a tool to help people be more focused in setting goals for spiritual health. It contains suggested goals, questions to think about, and a chart for keeping track of feedback from spiritual partners. Point it out and encourage group members to use it if it seems helpful. You may also want to consult your Small Group Calendar (page 69) to see who might lead your discussion next time.

In preparation for next week, ask someone in the group to bring a CD next time that contains a song they find especially meaningful for worship. You might have a different person share a song each week. Not everyone owns worship music, but those who do might want to share it with the group.

SESSION THREE:
SURRENDERING YOUR PAST

Goals of the Session

- To understand the breadth of areas of your past that you may need to surrender
- To identify one step you will take to surrender one area of your past to God

If you have a CD or a musician, consider beginning your meeting with one or two songs.

Question 1. This is a low-threat beginning for a discussion about the past. Be aware throughout this session that most people have areas of their past about which they are highly sensitive. Some people are ashamed of their families or of their sins. Some are proud of who they have been and resist the notion that their status or achievements might need to be surrendered. It will be helpful if you look at your own past ahead of time and set an example of a willingness to surrender something significant.

Question 2. Paul talks about his ethnic background, his religious heritage, his achievements, and his sin. He's neither embarrassed to talk about any of it nor prone to cling to any of it as his source of pride.

Question 7. The idea of embracing suffering is so alien to our culture that it's worth talking about. Suffering is not evidence that we're out of God's will or that God isn't doing his job. Suffering is part of life in a fallen world. Our option is either to suffer for the advancement of good in the world or to suffer fruitlessly. Suffering for the right reasons can actually bring us closer to Jesus in ways that nothing else can.

Question 8. Before you get into this question, be sure the group understands why surrendering our past to God is important. Sometimes our past immobilizes us and keeps us from living for God fully in the present. But once we offer an element of our past into God's hands, he can use it to bring good, both to us and to the world. This is true of sins, hurts, and strengths.

Questions 8 and 9 are difficult, because the things we most need to surrender are often the things we cling to most firmly. It was hard for the Jewish Christians of Paul's day to surrender their Jewishness to God—they were proud of being Jews, and rightly so. In the same way, it's hard for white middle-class Americans to imagine that their ethnic or social background needs to be surrendered. Obviously, surrendering these things doesn't mean ceasing to be white or middle class. It doesn't mean wallowing in the mire of political correctness. Likewise, surrendering one's African-American heritage doesn't mean there's anything wrong with being African-American. Nevertheless, modern politics make these very touchy issues. Help people understand that surrender in these areas simply means being open to letting God use these areas in whatever way he chooses.

Another potentially touchy issue is past sins. People may not want to tell the group about past sexual behavior, for example. That's fine. Allow your group to go as deep as is appropriate for the level of intimacy they've reached so far. Encourage them to find at least one person to talk to about a past sin that troubles them.

Many group members may want to focus on past hurts. It's easier to talk about hurts than sins or social status. You have a great opportunity to listen to people's pain and offer them comfort. Taking a step of forgiveness may be the most important area of surrender for many group members.

Question 9. Encourage group members to identify something specific they can do as an act of surrender. Taking action makes the theoretical real.

Question 13. It may be hard to save time for this conversation. If so, keep it for another meeting. However, don't forget about it, because it's an opportunity for members to begin to share ownership of the group. Some groups expect the leader to do everything, but healthy groups come to share responsibilities over time. By taking on small tasks like these, members will also discover and develop their gifts and interests with regard to serving others. Experimenting with acts of service will eventually help people identify how God has uniquely designed them for ministry. The suggested tasks are only ideas. Encourage group members to decide for themselves what would be good ways to serve the group. Ideally, get the group to go to the Purpose Team sheet (page 70). This will give a comprehensive understanding of the concept. You want to move forward with the presumption that each member will participate on a team or fill a role.

SESSION FOUR: SURRENDERING YOUR FUTURE

Goals of the Session

- To understand what surrendering your future involves
- To practice thankfulness as a way to strengthen your trust in God for your future

If you have a CD or a musician, consider beginning your meeting with one or two songs.

Question 2. Answers can range from the mundane to the spiritual. You may be certain that China exists, even though you've never seen it. You may be certain that God exists, even though you've never seen him.

Question 3. Noah was certain that God was going to wipe out humans in a huge flood because he believed God had told him so. It was a crazy thing to believe by today's standards. If one of your neighbors claimed that God told him something like this, you might well be skeptical.

Question 4. Noah invested a huge amount of time and money building the ark. If he had been wrong, it all would have been wasted. And once the rain started, Noah had to trust God to protect him and his family. The flood lasted for half a year (Genesis 7:24), and all this time Noah had to sit in the ark and trust God.

Question 5. God promised Abraham that he would have a whole nation of descendants who would own all of Palestine (Genesis 12:1–7). But he had to wait decades for even one son, and he died without owning more than a tiny plot of land.

Question 7. Invite group members to share experiences of having hoped for much and having received little.

Question 8. Revelation 21 describes the city.

Question 9. This is perhaps the most important question in the study. Allow people to share their concerns. Try to give equal airtime to everyone. If you have a member who tends to dominate the group with his or her concerns, you may need to say something gentle, such as, "Susan, this sounds like an important issue for us to pray about at the end of our meeting. Thanks so much for sharing it with us. What are some of the concerns on other persons' hearts?"

Ask people not to give advice about the issues shared by others. Instead, let the group's faith encourage each person to entrust each issue to God. Encouragement is generally more helpful than advice.

Some group members may be confused about what it means to surrender family members. Does it mean telling God it will be okay if our family members die? No. Sometimes our loved ones do die, and surrendering them means accepting the grief that comes with this loss. It also means surrendering any bitterness against God. But this kind of surrender usually takes time, and it never means saying that the death was "okay." Jesus treated others' deaths as a supreme outrage. On a more common level, surrendering our families means letting go of the drive to control what they do or how they turn out. It means taking responsibility for how we treat them and letting them take responsibility for the choices they make. Luke 15:11–32 depicts our heavenly Father surrendering his children to the consequences of their choices.

Question 12. Here's an opportunity for members who have never prayed aloud to give it a try. They have a script to work from, so they don't have to worry about coming up with words. If people are shy, reassure them that the point is not to impress each other with eloquent words. It's great to be thankful for the smallest things.

Question 13. Because people will be sharing concerns in question 9, you don't need to spend as much time on prayer concerns at this point. It's more important to invest your time actually praying.

SESSION FIVE:
SURRENDERING
YOUR SUBSTITUTES

Goals of the Session

- To understand what idolatry looks like in a modern setting
- To identify one false god you struggle with

We are often blind to the things we cling to for comfort, pain relief, and fulfillment—things that serve as a substitute for God. Also, many of these things are embarrassing to admit to. Workaholism is socially acceptable in our culture, but it will be a rare group where someone admits out of the blue to using Internet pornography or going on food binges to handle stress. For both of these reasons, the subject in this session is challenging for a small group discussion. It will be enormously helpful if you look at your own life ahead of time and think about what you do to for fulfillment or relief from pain. Do television or sports or romance novels play too big a role in your life?

False gods don't have to be classic addictions—drugs, for example—to be hindrances to our spiritual lives. If your group has trouble relating to the idea of idolatry, you could cast the discussion in terms of priorities that are out of order.

Question 1. It's okay if people can't come up with deeper answers than "yelling" or "grumbling." This is just a warm-up question. However, you will help the group if you reflect somewhat more deeply about yourself. Do you sometimes bury yourself in television watching in order to avoid uncomfortable feelings? Do you use shopping or ice cream as a comfort? In moderation, these stress relievers aren't necessarily sinful. And if you are overusing some pain relief strategy, wouldn't it be better to admit it to yourself?

Question 2. In a desert climate, water signifies the precious essential resource that makes life possible. It's the thing about which one can say, "I would die without. . . ." The human soul feels as though it is dying when it is denied love, a sense of being valued, a sense of being important enough to deserve to exist. Humiliation and meaninglessness are examples of feelings that make it appear to us as though we're dying. The water of the soul is what enables the soul to flourish.

Question 3. Worshiping an idol is creating your own supply of "water." When we seek feelings of importance, meaning, love, and security from something other than God, then we're seeking the water of the soul from something other than God.

Question 4. Frankly, God doesn't make us feel good all the time. He's more interested in nourishing our souls to become strong, tender, brave, and loving. To do that, he lets us face pain. It often feels as though he's depriving us of the water our souls need to survive. If pain relief is more important to us than character growth, we'll most often look to other sources of what feels to us like soul water.

Question 6. The big clue is the "I would die without. . . ." attitude. If someone looks to work as the source of feelings of fulfillment and importance to the degree that his or her relationships with God and others suffer, then work is becoming a false god.

Question 8. False gods make us feel better; the real God makes us better humans. False gods make our hearts hurt less; the real God makes our hearts bigger, more loving, more compassionate, more brave, more tender.

Question 9. Give people a minute to think about this question. Don't push for verbal responses, because this is a very embarrassing question. It will be great if you are willing to disclose an area where your priorities are off-kilter.

Goals of the Session

- To be motivated to surrender your whole life to God
- To celebrate the end of this study

Question 1. The point of this question is to allow group members to affirm the good memories they have of the group.

Question 2. The image suggests one's lifeblood poured out in total surrender to God, which is the supreme act of worship.

Question 3. The surrendered life isn't passive. Often it's uncomfortable. It's an active, strenuous, and rich life—rich in passion, in meaningfulness, in eternal impact and rewards.

Question 4. Paul believed that hearing Jesus' "well done!" in the next life would make his sufferings in this life entirely worth enduring. This attitude may be foreign to many group members. Heaven seems like a vague place, while the pains of the here and now are vivid. Talk about the idea of receiving a victor's crown from Jesus. How big a deal is it to your group members? Talk about what the victor's crown represents: an impact on the lives of human beings that will have a lasting impact into eternity. Because each human life matters eternally, the effect you have on someone's life now is of eternal value.

Question 6. Our culture avoids thinking about death. For some Christians, the thoroughly biblical teaching of Jesus' return becomes an excuse to avoid facing the possibility that they may die before Jesus comes again. Yet imagining our deaths can help us live for what really matters.

Question 7. You'll need paper and pens for this exercise. People won't come up with polished mission statements in a few minutes, but this exercise is a concrete way to start thinking about what they stand for. For example, if what you really stand for is revealing Jesus Christ's nature through all you do, then career and family goals can glide into perspective.

Question 8. Try to reserve ten minutes to review your Purpose-Driven Group Agreement. The end of a study is a chance to evaluate what has been good and what could be improved on in your group. It's a time for some people to bow out gracefully and for others to recommit for a new season. If you're planning to go on to another study in the DOING LIFE TOGETHER series, session 1 of that study will reintroduce the agreement. You don't have to discuss it again then if you do so now.

Question 11. Communion will probably take ten minutes if you have everything prepared ahead of time. It's a tremendously moving experience in a small group. Not all churches want their small groups to do Communion on their own, so if you're in doubt, be sure to check with your leadership. An extended time of musical worship with a CD or guitar is also a great way for people to surrender to God in worship.

Finally, consider planning a celebration to mark the end of this episode in your group. You might share a meal, go out for dessert, or plan a party for your next meeting.

ABOUT THE AUTHORS

Brett and Dee Eastman have served at Saddleback Valley Community Church since July 1997, after previously serving for five years at Willow Creek Community Church in Illinois. Brett's primary responsibilities are in the areas of small groups, strategic planning, and leadership development. Brett has earned his Masters of Divinity degree from Talbot School of Theology and his Management Certificate from Kellogg School of Business at Northwestern University. Dee is the real hero in the family, who, after giving birth to Joshua and Breanna, gave birth to identical triplets—Meagan, Melody, and Michelle. Dee is the coleader of the women's Bible study at Saddleback Church called "The Journey." They live in Las Flores, California.

Todd and Denise Wendorff have served at Saddleback Valley Community Church since 1998. Todd is a pastor in the Maturity Department at Saddleback, and Denise coleads a women's Bible class with Dee Eastman called "The Journey." Todd earned a Masters of Theology degree from Talbot School of Theology. He has taught Biblical Studies courses at Biola University, Golden Gate Seminary, and other universities. Previously, Todd and Denise served at Willow Creek Community Church. They love to help others learn to dig into God's Word for themselves and experience biblical truths in their lives. Todd and Denise live in Trabuco Canyon, California, with their three children, Brooke, Brittany, and Brandon.

Karen Lee-Thorp has written or cowritten more than fifty books, workbooks, and Bible studies. Her books include *A Compact Guide to the Christian Life*, *How to Ask Great Questions*, and *Why Beauty Matters*. She was a senior editor at NavPress for many years and series editor for the LifeChange Bible study series. She is now a freelance writer living in Brea, California, with her husband, Greg Herr, and their daughters, Megan and Marissa.

SMALL GROUP ROSTER

Name	Address	Phone	E-mail Address	Team or Role	Church Ministry
Bill Jones	7 Abralar street L.F. 92665	766-2255	bjones@aol.com	socials	children's ministry

Be sure to pass your booklets around the room the first night, or have someone volunteer to type the group roster for all members. Encourage group ownership by having each member share a team role or responsibility.

Name	Address	Phone	E-mail Address	Team or Role	Church Ministry

Doing Life Together series

BRETT & DEE EASTMAN; KAREN LEE-THORP;
DENISE & TODD WENDORFF

ased on the five biblical purposes that form the bedrock of Saddleback Church, Doing Life Together will help your group discover what God created you for and how you can turn this dream into an everyday reality. Experience the transformation firsthand as you begin Connecting, Growing, Developing, Sharing, and Surrendering your life together for him.

"Doing Life Together is a groundbreaking study ... [It's] the first small group curriculum built completely on the purpose-driven paradigm ... The greatest reason I'm excited about [it] is that I've seen the dramatic changes it produces in the lives of those who study it."

—FROM THE FOREWORD BY RICK WARREN

Small Group Ministry Consultation

Building a healthy, vibrant, and growing small group ministry is challenging. That's why Brett Eastman and a team of certified coaches are offering small group ministry consultation. Join pastors and church leaders from around the country to discover new ways to launch and lead a healthy Purpose-Driven small group ministry in your church. To find out more information please call 1-888-467-1977.

Curriculum Kit	ISBN: 0-310-25002-1
Beginning Life Together	ISBN: 0-310-24672-5 Softcover
	ISBN: 0-310-25004-8 DVD
Connecting with God's Family	ISBN: 0-310-24673-3 Softcover
	ISBN: 0-310-25005-6 DVD
Growing to Be Like Christ	ISBN: 0-310-24674-1 Softcover
	ISBN: 0-310-25006-4 DVD
Developing Your SHAPE to Serve Others	ISBN: 0-310-24675-X Softcover
	ISBN: 0-310-25007-2 DVD
Sharing Your Life Mission Every Day	ISBN: 0-310-24676-8 Softcover
	ISBN: 0-310-25008-0 DVD
Surrendering Your Life for God's Pleasure	ISBN: 0-310-24677-6 Softcover
	ISBN: 0-310-25009-9 DVD

ZONDERVAN™

GRAND RAPIDS, MICHIGAN 49530 USA

WWW.ZONDERVAN.COM

life**together**.com

The Purpose-Driven® Life
WHAT ON EARTH AM I HERE FOR?

RICK WARREN

The most basic question everyone faces in life is *Why am I here? What is my purpose?* Self-help books suggest that people should look within, at their own desires and dreams, but Rick Warren says the starting place must be with God — and his eternal purposes for each life. Real meaning and significance comes from understanding and fulfilling God's purposes for putting us on earth.

The Purpose-Driven Life takes the groundbreaking message of the award-winning *Purpose-Driven Church* and goes deeper, applying it to the lifestyle of individual Christians. This book helps readers understand God's incredible plan for their lives. Warren enables them to see "the big picture" of what life is all about and begin to live the life God created them to live.

The Purpose-Driven Life is a manifesto for Christian living in the 21st century — a lifestyle based on eternal purposes, not cultural values. Using biblical stories and letting the Bible speak for itself, Warren clearly explains God's 5 purposes for each of us:

We were planned for God's pleasure — experience real worship.
We were formed for God's family — enjoy real fellowship.
We were created to become like Christ — learn real discipleship.
We were shaped for serving God — practice real ministry.
We were made for a mission — live out real evangelism.

This long-anticipated book is the life-message of Rick Warren, founding pastor of Saddleback Church. Written in a captivating devotional style, the book is divided into 40 short chapters that can be read as a daily devotional, studied by small groups, and used by churches participating in the nationwide "40 Days of Purpose" campaign.

Hardcover: 0-310-20571-9   Unabridged Audio Pages® CD: 0-310-24788-8
                                        Unabridged Audio Pages® cassette: 0-310-20907-2

Also available from Inspirio, the gift division of Zondervan

Purpose-Driven Life Journal: 0-310-80306-3
Planned for God's Pleasure (Gift Book):   0-310-80322-5
ScriptureKeeper® Plus Purpose-Driven® Life: 0-310-80323-3

We want to hear from you. Please send your comments about this book to us in care of the address below. Thank you.

ZONDERVAN™

GRAND RAPIDS, MICHIGAN 49530 USA

WWW.ZONDERVAN.COM